Early Writing Program

LESSON GUIDE

Donna Reid Connell

AGS®
American Guidance Service
Circle Pines, Minnesota 55014-1796

Originally published as *itl Integrated Total Language*
©1978 by Academic Therapy Publications, Inc.
ISBN: 0-88671-197-5

CONTENTS

Preface 5

Introduction 7

    Organization 10

    Materials 13

    General Directions for Using *itl* Lessons 14

        Classroom Organization 14

        Stories 15

        Animal Drawings 15

        Dictation Activities 16

        Check Point 16

        Extended Activities 16

Lessons 19

    Unit 1: Getting Ready to Write 21

    Unit 2: *itl* in the Garden (*i,t,l*) 35

    Unit 3: *itl* in the Meadow (*j, c, a, d, g, f, s, o*) 63

    Unit 4: *itl* at the Farm (*e,u,r,n,h,m,p,b,qu,ng*) 109

    Unit 5: *itl* and *hamilton hound* (*th, ch, sh, th*) 151

    Unit 6: *itl* Goes Camping (long-vowel sounds) 167

    Unit 7: *itl* at the Zoo (*k,y,w,v,x,z*) 175

    Unit 8: Alphabet Order and Capital Letters 201

Appendixes 207

    Appendix A: Signing Alphabet 209

    Appendix B: Materials 210

    Appendix C: Letter and Sound Chart 211

PREFACE

efore Dr. James Allen's tragic death in 1970, I was inspired by his appeal to the nation for a restructuring of our public education system to emphasize the importance of the early childhood years. He believed that every child should have the right to read and that this could be best accomplished with home and school working together.

Through an intensive search of professional literature, combining the research of Maria Montessori, Rhoda Kellogg, Keith Beery, and others, I discovered that young children's drawing develops the visual and physical readiness for writing, which then often explodes spontaneously into early reading.

I am grateful to my youngest child, Mike, who at age four pointed the way to using drawing as the beginning of literacy instruction. Mike showed me how to cartoon alphabet letters into animals and how to make up stories about the letter animals related to their speech sounds. His invention provided me with an ideal system for developing hand-eye coordination, visual imagery, and sound-symbol relationships with activities suitable for young children.

My long-term field study using Mike's system to encourage early drawing and writing took ten years. It would not have been possible without the encouragement of my husband, John, and the support of our county school superintendent, Floyd Seifert, who approved field projects associated with my work as a reading specialist.

I am grateful to the hundreds of parents and teachers throughout the United States who used my experimental materials. Special thanks go to the twenty kindergarten teachers who tried an early edition of my early writing program for a full school year. Their feedback provided valuable information that confirmed my belief that restoring writing to its former place in American schools through early education at home and school can make a significant improvement in American literacy.

My observations of early drawing and writing have led me to believe that they not only lead to successful early reading but also promote more organized thinking. Drawing and writing enhance visual imagery, leading to better reading comprehension. They also provide a vehicle for expressing feelings, leading to better mental health.

Most of all, I thank the thousands of young children who have shown me the way.

Donna Reid Connell
January 1985

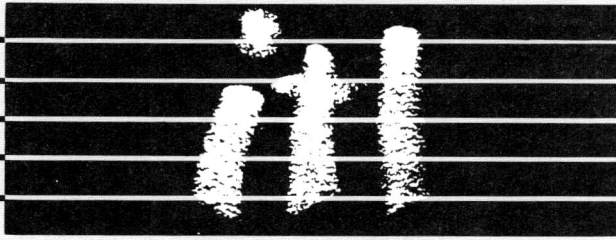

INTRODUCTION

Introduction

The *itl Early Writing Program* shows young children how to make alphabet letters and how to make the speech sounds associated with the letters. *itl* lessons and activities implement the philosophy and research described in the book *Writing Is Child's Play.* The program teaches a simplified form of lowercase, continuous-line letters and gives special emphasis to writing as a means of communicating with other people. The lessons systematically teach young children writing and phonics skills and promote original composition.

The *itl* program is appropriate for use with preschool, kindergarten, or first-grade children in whole class or small group settings. It has also been successfully used by parents in one-to-one teaching at home. The lessons can be adapted for use with children from ages three to eight or with children functioning at these age levels regardless of their age.

The program uses a multisensory approach that reflects children's natural neurological development. As in oral language development, written language must be introduced with both expressive and receptive activities. Communication is a two-way process. Each sound and symbol is introduced in a sequence of auditory, oral, tactile, kinetic, and visual experiences. First children hear the letter sound in a story about an animal character, for example, *molly* mosquito humming. They are led to make the sound, discovering the parts of the vocal mechanism used to produce it and feeling the sound while they hear themselves make it. Next, they "write" the animal's letter in the air, imitating the teacher to ensure the correct stroke sequence. Children then write the letter with a writing tool (soft-lead pencil, black writing crayon, or black felt-tipped pen). They are shown how to draw the animal around the letter. Finally, they are shown the letter alone and asked to articulate its speech sound. This sequence is suitable for young children because it starts with what is known (the speech sound already used) and works toward the unknown (the letter) through low-level, active involvement.

Lessons in the *itl* program are sequential. Letters are introduced one at a time, grouped according to their writing difficulty for young children. Letters made with vertical and horizontal strokes—*i, t,* and *l*—are introduced first. Letters oriented toward the left are second: *j, c, a, d, g, f, s,* and *o.* Letters that are oriented toward the right are next. First *e* and *u* are introduced, and then letters that begin with a vertical line followed by a right curve: *r, n, h, m, p,* and *b.* The rounded form of the letters *y* and *w* are next. Finally the lowercase letters with diagonal strokes, are introduced—*k, v, x,* and *z;* these are the most difficult letters for young children to make.

The digraphs *qu, ng, th* (voiced and unvoiced), *ch, sh,* and the words *a* and *the* are also introduced.

As children learn the letters and their most common sounds, they begin to write words, phrases, and sentences, first from dictation of sounds by others and then by dictating original compositions to themselves.

Each letter is introduced first with its most frequently used sound.[*]

---

[*]Information on the relative frequencies of sounds in words is based on *Relative Frequency of English Spellings,* by Godfrey Dewey (New York: Teachers College Press, 1970).

Short-vowel sounds are introduced before long-vowel sounds because they are more common in English. Alphabet order, letter names, and capital letters are added after children have mastered the basic concepts of writing with lowercase letters. The simplest spelling rules are introduced as the need arises, but invented phonetic spelling is encouraged in early original compositions until the spelling rules can be followed.

ORGANIZATION

The 59 lessons in the *itl* program are organized into eight units as follows:

Unit 1: **Getting Ready to Write**

This unit is devoted to establishing cues for left-to-right progression and to teaching children to write their own two initials so they can label their papers.

Lesson 1. To recognize the color green as a *GO* signal.

Lesson 2. To associate *green* and *go* with the left side.

Lesson 3. To associate *red* and *stop* with the right side.

Lesson 4. To identify three-dimensional objects represented by two-dimensional images.

Lesson 5. To write the initials of one's first and last names.

Unit 2: itl **at the Garden**

The adventures of *itl* inchworm and his letter animal friends begin in this unit. The letters *i*, *t*, and *l* are introduced. Sound blending and writing letters from sound dictation are also introduced.

Lesson 6. To recognize the letter *i*, to say its short-vowel sound, as in *it*, and to write the letter correctly.

Lesson 7. To recognize and draw vertical and horizontal lines.

Lesson 8. To recognize the letter *t*, to say its speech sound, and to write the letter correctly.

Lesson 9. To blend the sounds /i/ and /t/ into the word *it*.*

Lesson 10. To recognize the letter *l*, to say its speech sound, and to write the letter correctly.

Lesson 11. To blend the sounds /l/, /i/, and /t/ into words and to write the words from dictation.

Lesson 12. To blend the letters *i*, *t*, and *l* into the names *itl*, *lit*, and *til*, and to write the words from dictation.

Lesson 13. To review letters and speech sounds for *i*, *t*, and *l*, and to review the words *it*, *lit*, *itl*, and *til*.

---

*When letters are enclosed in slashes in the text, they refer to the *speech* sounds represented by the letters. When letters are italicized in the text, they refer to alphabet letter *names*, as in *a*, *b*, *c*.

Unit 3: *itl* at the Meadow

Letters that have left-curve strokes are introduced. The letter *j* combines a vertical stroke with a left-curve stroke, to provide a transition from the Unit 2 letters. The letters *c, a, d, g, f, s,* and *o* start with left-curve strokes.

Lesson 14. To recognize the letter *j*, to say its speech sound, and to write the letter correctly.

Lesson 15. To recognize the letter *c*, to say its hard sound, as in *music* and *cat,* and to write the letter correctly.

Lesson 16. To recognize the letter *a*, to say its short-vowel sound, as in *at,* and to write the letter correctly.

Lesson 17. To recognize the letter *d*, to say its speech sound, as in *sad,* and to write the letter correctly.

Lesson 18. To recognize the letter *g*, to say its sound, as in *dog,* and to write the letter correctly.

Lesson 19. To review the letters and sounds *i, t, l, j, c, a, d, g,* to write words from dictation using these letters, and to read the words.

Lesson 20. To recognize the letter *f*, to say its sound, and to write the letter correctly.

Lesson 21. To recognize the letter *s*, to say its sound, as in *cats,* and to write the letter correctly.

Lesson 22. To make the /s/ sound, as in *is,* and to distinguish it from the /s/ sound in *cats.*

Lesson 23. To recognize the letter *o*, to say its short-vowel sound, as in *on,* and to write the letter correctly.

Lesson 24. To make the /o/ sound, as in *off,* and to distinguish it from the /o/ sound in *on.*

Lesson 25. To discriminate the four speech sounds for the letter *o* (*on, off, go, to*).

Unit 4: *itl* at the Farm

Letters that are oriented toward the right—*e, u, r, n, h, m, p, b*—are introduced. Numerals oriented to the right—1 - 5—are included, and children can practice writing on wide-lined paper, depending on their writing development. The digraphs *qu* and *ng* are also introduced in this unit.

Lesson 26. To recognize the letter *e*, to say its short-vowel sound, as in *edge,* and to write the letter correctly.

Lesson 27. To recognize numbers 1 - 5, to tell their values, and to write the numerals correctly.

Lesson 28. To place letters correctly on wide-lined paper.

Lesson 29. To recognize the letter *u*, to say its short-vowel sound, as in *up,* and to write the letter correctly.

Lesson 30. To draw rainbow curves from left to right.

Lesson 31. To recognize the letter *r*, to say its speech sound, and to write the letter correctly.

Lesson 32. To recognize the letter *n*, to say its speech sound, and to write the letter correctly.

Lesson 33. To recognize the letter *h*, to say its speech sound, and to write the letter correctly.

Lesson 34. To recognize the letter *m*, to say its speech sound, and to write the letter correctly.

Lesson 35. To recognize the letter *p*, to say its speech sound, as in *up*, and to write the letter correctly.

Lesson 36. To recognize the letter *b*, to say its sound, as in *tub*, and to write the letter correctly.

Lesson 37. To recognize the digraph *qu*, to say its sound, and to write *qu* correctly from dictation.

Lesson 38. To recognize the digraph *ng*, to say its sound, and to write *ng* correctly from dictation.

Unit 5: *itl* and *hamilton hound*

The digraphs *th* (voiced and unvoiced), *ch*, *sh*, the words *a* and *the*, and numerals 6 - 10 are introduced.

Lesson 39. To recognize the word *a*, to pronounce the word (*uh*), and to write the word correctly.

Lesson 40. To recognize the voiced digraph *th*, to say its sound, as in *this*, and to write *th* in words.

Lesson 41. To recognize the word *the*, to say the word with the unvoiced *schwa* sound for *e* (thuh), and to write the word correctly.

Lesson 42. To recognize the digraph *ch*, to say its sound, as in *itch*, and to write *ch* in words.

Lesson 43. To recognize the digraph *sh*, to say its sound, and to write *sh* in words.

Lesson 44. To recognize and write the numerals 6 - 10.

Lesson 45. To recognize the unvoiced digraph *th* sound, as in *bath*, and to distinguish it from the voiced digraph *th* as in *this*.

Unit 6: *itl* Goes Camping

Long-vowel sounds and spelling cues for long-vowel sounds are presented.

Lesson 46. To say the alphabet names for the vowels *a, e, i, o, u*.

Lesson 47. To recognize that an *e* at the end of the word is often a cue for a long-vowel sound.

Lesson 48. To recognize that double-vowel patterns are often cues for long-vowel sounds.

Unit 7: *itl* at the Zoo

The last two right-curve letters, *w* and *y*, and the letters with diagonal strokes, *k, v, x, z*, are introduced.

Lesson 49. To recognize the letter *k*, to say its speech sound, and to write the letter correctly.

Lesson 50. To use the letters *c* and *k* correctly in spelled words: *c* before *a, o,* and *u,* and *k* before *i* and *e.*

Lesson 51. To use the endings *ke* and *ck* correctly.

Lesson 52. To recognize the letter *y,* to say its sound, as in *happy,* and to write the letter correctly.

Lesson 53. To make the /y/ sound, as in *my,* and to distinguish it from the /y/ sound in *happy.*

Lesson 54. To recognize the letter *w,* to say its sound, as in *few,* and to write the letter correctly.

Lesson 55. To recognize the letter *v,* to say its sound, as in *have,* and to write the letter correctly.

Lesson 56. To recognize the letter *x,* to say its sound, as in *six,* and to write the letter correctly.

Lesson 57. To recognize the letter *z,* to say its sound, and to write the letter correctly.

Unit 8: **Alphabet Order and Capital Letters**

Children say and write the alphabet in order and learn to write capital letters.

Lesson 58. To say and write the alphabet in order.

Lesson 59. To recognize, use, and write capital letters correctly.

MATERIALS

The following materials are included in the *itl Early Writing Program:*

Writing Is Child's Play—a book that describes the program philosophy and suggests ways for parents and teachers to nurture young children's natural drive to write. It includes background information on letter forms, primary spelling rules, and phonics, as well as related research.

Lesson Guide—a comprehensive manual that gives detailed instructions for teaching the *itl* lessons. Each lesson includes an objective, background about the letter or sound being taught, an activity or story and related activity, an informal evaluation, and extended activities to reinforce the lesson.

Character Cards—28 full-color cards that illustrate the 26 animal characters and letter forms, with two additional character stories. The cards are 8″ x 8″. The stories are printed on the backs of the cards as well as in the *Lesson Guide.*

itl puppet—a green and yellow sock puppet that represents the letter *i* and the sound "ih." The *itl* stories are based on the adventures of *itl* and his 25 letter-animal friends. The puppet may be used to introduce *itl* activities and to tell the stories.

Poster—a full-color poster that shows the 26 letter animals in their various settings—garden, meadow, farm, zoo. The poster may be displayed in the classroom and used to review letters and sounds. It can also be used to review the continuing story as new stories are told.

Audiocassette—recordings of 28 *itl* stories to model the speech sounds for parents or teachers. The recordings may also be used to present the stories to children as the character cards are shown.

my itl book—a student book that includes a tear-out activity for drawing each of the *itl* letter animals around its alphabet letter. When the drawing activities have been removed from the book, the child will have a skinny *itl* book that includes the pictures and sounds for all 26 animal characters. One book is included with the *itl Early Writing Program;* additional books may be ordered.

Blackline Masters—84 masters that may be either duplicated on a photocopying machine or transferred to a ditto master for duplication on a ditto machine.

> a Progress Checklist for recording individual student progress
>
> a lesson planning and evaluation form for teachers
>
> 69 activity sheets for use in the lessons
>
> 13 parent letters to inform parents about the program and to give them the opportunity to reinforce children's writing skills at home

Tello Cards—54 small black-and-white cards that contain illustrations of the letter animals. The cards can be used in a "concentration"-type matching game that gives children practice making sounds and matching sounds and letters.

Sample writing materials suitable for young children are included with the *itl Early Writing Program.* Additional writing materials may be ordered.

> one black writing crayon
>
> one triangular plastic pencil gripper
>
> one soft-lead pencil
>
> one wipe-off writing slate

Carrying Case—All *itl* materials are contained in a heavy cardboard carrying case with a plastic handle and Velcro closures.

GENERAL DIRECTIONS FOR USING *itl* LESSONS

Each of the 59 lessons in the *Lesson Guide* has an objective, an "Understandings" section that includes background information for parents or teachers, a materials list, an activity or story and activity, and an evaluation check point. In addition, extended activities include a variety of activities that reinforce the lesson and give children additional practice with letters and sounds.

It is important that adults adapt the program to the developmental levels of the children being taught. For example, very young three-year-olds will enjoy the stories. They can retell the stories in their own words, can recognize the letter animals, and can practice making specific speech sounds. To build visual imagery and hand-eye coordination for later writing, these children should have a period of free drawing every day. They should be encouraged to draw with a black felt-tipped pen or with a black crayon. When the drawing or scribbling design is complete, they can color it. Painting or other art projects aren't a substitute for drawing with a writing tool.

Following are suggestions and guidelines for presenting *itl* activities.

Classroom Organization

For all *itl* letter-writing activities, students must be facing in the same direction. Learning the correct direction and sequence of letter strokes is vital to fluent writing. If children face each other during beginning letter-writing activities, any reversal tendencies they have will be reinforced. For drawing or letter-writing activities in which the teacher demonstrates actions or drawing, the teacher should also be facing in the same direction as the students. The Letter and Sound Chart in Appendix C shows the stroke sequences and speech sounds for each letter.

Unit 1 lessons are devoted to introducing cues that will help familiarize children with the top-to-bottom, left-to-right patterns of written English. A green *GO* circle on the left side of the room or writing area and an octagonal red *STOP* sign on the right side are introduced in Unit 1 and referred to throughout the program.

Stories

Each of the 26 letter animals and its corresponding sound is introduced in a short story. The stories may be presented by reading them from the *Lesson Guide* or character card or by playing the recorded story. Teachers or parents who read the stories may want to listen to the letter sound on the recorded version before telling the stories, to check their own sound production. The Phonics Guide in *Writing Is Child's Play* will also help to isolate single-letter sounds. The average length of the stories is one-and-a-half to two-and-a-half minutes.

There is a full-color character card for each of the 26 letter animals. These are displayed during the story presentations to help children begin to associate the letters, letter animals, and their related sounds.

At the kindergarten level, it is usually best to begin with one letter a week, reinforcing the letter and sound daily with varied multisensory activities. By Unit 3, children can learn two letters a week, then three letters a week for Units 4 through 7. As with any program, some children will need additional reinforcement. However, this will be minimized if a variety of multisensory activities that covers children's major learning modes is being used.

The *itl* program has been used successfully with children whose home language is not English. When the short stories are translated into another language, the animal sounds don't change. For example, the mosquito character built around the letter *m* still hums "m-m-m-m" even though the insect may be called a different name.

Following each story in which a new sound and letter are introduced, children are asked to make the sound and to write the letter in the air. The teacher demonstrates by making the sound and writing the letter in the air using whole-arm movements. Then children repeat the sound while writing the letter in the air several times. Information about placement of the tongue and lips for producing the sounds is included, along with suggestions for helping children who are having difficulty making a particular sound.

Animal Drawings

After listening to the story, saying the sound, and writing the letter in the air, children draw a simplified illustration of the animal character. For each new sound and letter there is a drawing activity in *my itl book* that contains the same letter as on the character card, without the animal features.

The teacher demonstrates a step-by-step drawing of the animal character on a large sheet of newsprint, and children follow each step, drawing the animal around its letter. For these drawing activities, children draw the animal outlines with black crayon. Then children are shown how to make the animal's "talking balloon" and write the letter in the balloon. Once the pictures are outlined, children color their picture.

The *my itl book* drawing activities are perforated; they should be removed from the book and the separate sheet given to each child. If the sheets are left in the book, children may try to copy the animal illustration on the remaining portion of the page.

Dictation Activities

Beginning in Unit 2, after several letters have been introduced, sound dictation is begun. In these activities, children write the alphabet letter with no copy in sight in response to hearing the teacher make the sound. As children learn more letters, the dictation exercises include two- and three-letter words and sentences.

When more than one sound is being dictated, holding up a finger for each sound will help children know whether they have included all the letters dictated. Saying "space" at the end of each word will help children learn to space between words. Right-handed children should be encouraged to leave a two-finger-wide space between words. Left-handed children can be given a 1″-wide tagboard strip to measure word spaces. Children should not be expected to begin sentences with capital letters until after capitals are taught and rules for capitalization are introduced. Children are encouraged to use periods as stop signs at the end of sentences.

Check Point

At the end of each lesson, there is an informal evaluation to check each child's ability to make the speech sound and to write the letter in a correct stroke sequence. A Progress Checklist for recording individual growth is included with the blackline masters.

Each child should be asked to make the new sound when shown the letter and to write the letter without copying it when the sound is dictated. The letter can be written in the air, on a chalkboard, or on paper. Children who are having difficulty making the sound or writing the letter can be given individual help.

Extended Activities

A variety of follow-up activities for reinforcing the lesson and giving children additional practice writing letters and making sounds is included with most *itl* lessons. Many of these activities can be incorporated into other areas of the regular program or used in learning centers. They include drawing and coloring activities, games, finger spelling, dictation, role playing, activities that build hand-eye coordination, and activities that enhance gross motor development.

Tello Cards
The Tello Cards included in the *itl* kit contain small blackline drawings of the letter animals. In the lessons, these cards are used in a matching game in which children match the cards and *say* the letter sounds. The cards are arranged face down in

rows. The first player turns over two cards, saying each animal's sound. If the cards match, the child gets to keep them. If the cards don't match, the child returns them to their original places. The second player does the same. Each player tries to remember where the cards are so that she or he can match pairs. The player who keeps the most pairs wins the game. If children play this game by matching the pictures silently, they should be reminded that this is a *telling* game.

The cards should be kept in orderly rows during the game. A Tello board with outlines to show card placement can be made from cardboard, or an over-turned cardboard box can be used as a Tello table.

Look-and-Do Strips

Look-and-Do strips are used in the *itl* program to model reading; they teach the left-to-right, top-to-bottom pattern of written English. Look-and-Do strips that illus-trate action responses are introduced in Unit 1. The sequence of pictures tells chil-dren what to do and in what order. As letters are introduced, the strips are used to have children read single sounds represented by the letters and then to blend let-ters into voiced syllables and meaningful words.

To make the Look-and-Do strips, use strips of tagboard. The size of the strips will vary, depending on whether they are used in small or large groups or for one-to-one teaching. Color a green *GO* spot on the upper-left corner of each strip and a red *STOP* spot in the lower-right corner.

Continue to make Look-and-Do strips until all the lowercase letters are taught. Here are some examples of illustrated strips, strips that elicit single sounds, and strips that can be used in blending activities.

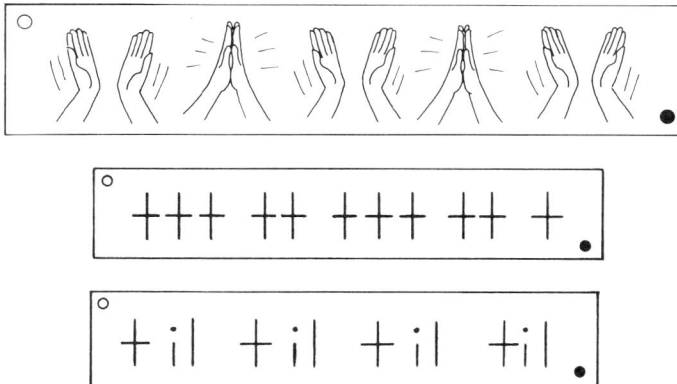

When presenting a strip to a group, moving your hand slowly across the bottom of the strip from the children's left to right will help children follow the strip and stay together. The strips can be posted where children can read them alone or in pairs. When several strips are used, they should be displayed under each other on a vertical surface so that children practice moving their eyes back to the left side as they finish each strip.

Finger Spelling

Finger spelling is enjoyed by children whether or not they are hearing impaired. Many of the finger letters resemble the alphabet letters they represent. The finger spelling activities require no equipment and take very little time. They are excellent activities when children are ready to go home or waiting for a bell to ring. The hand signals shown in the lessons and in Appendix A at the back of this guide show the hand turned toward the person doing the finger spelling. Once the letter is learned, the hand needs to be turned toward the person reading the signal.

Dramatic Play

Role playing, or informal dramatization, builds on the natural play of young children. Just as children pretend to be adults when they play house or store, they can be encouraged to replay the *itl* stories.

Adults may want to introduce dramatic play activities by rereading the story and having children pantomime the actions. Some coaching may be necessary to keep the action going. The *itl* character cards or the stick puppets made from the activity sheets may be used as props during the story enactments.

Children may enjoy representing the animal characters by forming the letter shapes with their body. For example, to form *itl*'s lowercase *i*, a child might stand straight with feet together and one arm at his or her side and raise the other hand with a closed fist to make the dot. For the letter *t*, children can stand straight and hold both arms straight out.

Gradually, children will be able to replay each story, taking the parts of the letter animals and using their own words for dialogue. Choosing outgoing children to present the first dramatizations will help model the activities for children who are more reserved. After watching their classmates, these children may be more likely to volunteer.

LESSONS

1 GETTING READY TO WRITE

nit 1 introduces direction and discrimination skills beginners need before they begin to write letters and words. Even when children are able to draw and understand written symbols, they need to learn to discriminate top from bottom and left from right on the writing surface. To help children become familiar with left-to-right progression, a green *GO* sign is placed in the room to the children's left and a red *STOP* sign to their right. These signs are used until later in the program when children are ready to substitute the words *left* and *right*. Children are also given practice identifying three-dimensional objects from two-dimensional illustrations. The Look-and-Do strips used in this unit are recommended throughout the *itl Early Writing Program.*

In addition, children learn to write their initials so they can label their work independently before some of them are able to write their full name.

Clues to writing readiness and additional information on preparing a writing environment for young children are included in Part 1 of *Writing Is Child's Play.*

LESSON 1

Objective To recognize the color green as a *GO* signal.

Understandings Letters have a distinct orientation to left or right. A feeling for *laterality*—the distinction between the left and right sides—is necessary for success in learning how to recognize and make alphabet letters. Laterality is often undeveloped in young children because the two sides of the body are mirror images of each other. The English language compounds the problem. Until children begin school, they usually associate the word *left* with what is *left over*. ("There's a little milk *left* in your glass.") Also, they often associate *right* with what is correct. Using these same words when teaching laterality confuses young children and slows down their laterality learning. It makes more sense to teach the *concept* of sides first, then add the vocabulary.

For itl letter-teaching activities, all students must be facing in the same direction. If children face each other across a table, they will reinforce any reversal tendencies they may already have. Although the lessons in Unit 1 do not teach letter-writing, it may be useful to organize your classroom environment so that students will be facing in the same direction during all itl activities.

Materials

3″ round cardboard templates (lids from cottage cheese containers will work), one per child

manila construction paper—9″ x 12″ sheets

GO sign—large, green paper circle (at least 8″ in diameter)

green crayons, one per child

scissors

staplers

tongue depressors (optional), one per child

Preparation

Place the *GO* sign to the students' left of the teaching area. The *GO* sign should be displayed during all *itl* lessons. If children do their writing in a different area, put another *GO* sign in the writing area, to the children's left.

This activity will go more smoothly if helpers are available to help students make the *GO* signs.

Activity

Begin a safety discussion by asking children to identify safety rules. For example: *"What safety rules do you follow when you ride in the school bus? in a car? when you walk to school?"*

Point out the big *GO* sign, asking children what green means on a traffic light. Emphasize that green means *go.* Then explain that each child is going to make a *GO* sign.

Demonstrate how to make a *GO* sign:

- Lay circle template near the edge of a piece of manila paper. Hold the template firmly with one hand while you draw around it with the other, using a green crayon.
- Color the circle green, staying inside the outline.
- Cut out the green circle.
- Fold the rest of the paper into a "stick" about 1″ wide. (You may substitute tongue depressors.)
- Staple the *GO* sign to the stick.

Give each child a template, construction paper, and a green crayon. Help children make their own *GO* signs. Write the children's initials for their first and last names on the backs of the signs using correct letter formation. (If helpers are to write the names, give them a copy of the capital letters you will use for initials; see Lesson 5.) Children who finish their signs quickly can color the other side of the circle, as well as the stick.

Check Point

As students are working, go around to each child and ask the color of the *GO* sign and what it tells us to do. Accept other words for *green* from children for whom English is a second language.

Children who don't know the names of the eight colors in a small crayon box (blue, red, yellow, green, brown, black, orange, purple) should be helped individually. This can be done by working with one child at a time, telling the child the names of two distinct colors, asking her or him to identify the (green) crayon, and then to tell the color. No more than three colors should be taught at a time.

Record individual performance on the Progress Checklist.

Extended Activities

1. Introduce a song or rhyme about the color green such as the first verse of this song.

D. Chapman

1. Green green, look for green. Green is an ol - ive and a
2. Red, red, look for red. Red is a ber - ry, a

fresh string - bean. Green is the col - or that tells us to go,
bright red ber - ry. Red is the col - or that tells us to stop,

And the jol - ly green gi - ant, ho, ho, ho!
— Red is the col - or of cher - ry pop.

23

2. Take a walk outdoors to look for green things. Compare the different shades of green in growing things.

3. Include green foods as a snack-time treat. Children will have fun popping, counting, and eating fresh green peas in a pod. Try crisp sticks of raw zucchini, celery sticks, bell pepper slices, cucumber or pickle slices. Encourage children to taste unfamiliar foods.

4. Use a *GO* sign as a nonverbal signal for children to move between activities and at dismissal.

5. Play a game with the *GO* signs. Tell children you are going to name some things that are green and some things that are not green. If what you name could be green, they are to raise their signs. If what you name is not green, they are not to raise the signs. For example:

grass	apples	paste
trees	snow	chocolate
bicycles	people	carrots
houses	dogs	

6. Send home Parent Letter 1.

Objective To associate *green* and *go* with the left side.

Understandings To lay the foundation skills for written English, young children need to know the beginning side and the ending side of each letter, word, and row of print. By labeling these the *GO* side and the *STOP* side, and by giving them color cues (green and red, the familiar traffic signal colors), children can start with what they already know. They must internalize the left-right distinction within their own body before they are able to apply it to tasks outside of themselves. It may take weeks of practice before each child can make an automatic response. (Many adults must still stop and think on left-right tasks because this was not carefully taught in their early years.)

Give extra attention to left-handed children when working on the *GO* and *STOP* activities. Drawing from left to right is a pull activity for right-handers, but a push activity for left-handers. Pushing the writing tool is harder than pulling it. (Review the sections "Children with Special Needs" and "Developing Thinking Skills" in Part 1 of *Writing Is Child's Play*.)

Materials

Activity Sheets 1 and 2, one copy of each per child
crayons—black and green for each child
paste
scissors

Activity

Display Activity Sheet 1, making sure the circles are on the children's left side. Explain that the circles are *GO* signs. Then ask children what color the *GO* signs should be.

Color the three circles green.

Tell children you are going to draw roads on the paper, starting at the *GO* signs. Using a black crayon, draw a horizontal line across the paper from each green circle.

Show Activity Sheet 2 and demonstrate how to cut out the cars on the dotted lines. Move a car along one of the roads, starting at the *GO* sign.

Distribute the activity sheets, crayons, and scissors. Show children how to hold a crayon with the thumb and middle finger, the pointer finger resting on top.

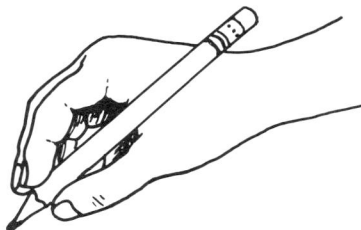

Have children complete the activity sheets independently. Some children may need help in holding the crayon correctly. Make note of any child who turns the activity sheet to make vertical rather than horizontal "roads." Children who avoid making horizontal lines will have difficulty learning to make letters. If necessary, tape their papers to a tabletop and give them extra practice with horizontal lines at an easel or chalkboard. (Review "Midline Difficulty" in *Writing Is Child's Play.*)

When children have moved their cars along the roads several times, have them paste the cars on Activity Sheet 1 beside the *GO* signs.

Check Point

While students are working, ask individuals to show you the *GO* side of their paper and to show you which way the cars are going.

Record individual performance on the Progress Checklist.

Extended Activities

1. Play "Simon Says." Mark the back of each child's left hand with a washable, non-toxic, green felt-tipped pen, or have children wear yarn pompom wristbands. Have children stand facing in the same direction. Tell them they are to follow instructions that begin with the words "Simon Says," but they are not to follow instructions that don't begin with those words. Give a number of instructions that require the use of the *GO* side, for example:

Simon says, put your *GO* hand behind you.
Simon says, turn around two times.
Simon says, lift your *GO* foot.
Touch your chin.

The last command was not preceded by the words "Simon Says," so children who *do* perform this command must sit down until the game is over.

2. When reading to children or calling roll, occasionally run your fingers under a line of print from left to right. Ask the children to imitate you, pointing to the beginning side (*GO* side), then making an invisible line in the air from left to right.

3. Send home Parent Letter 2.

LESSON 3

Objective To associate *red* and *stop* with the right side.

Understandings The left-to-right pattern of written English is a *taught* skill. Unless it becomes an automatic, subconscious response, a child will be handicapped in reading and writing activities. It is a handicap to stop and think, "left-right, left-right," before starting to write or read anything. Children who find this concept particularly difficult should be given individual help. (Review Part 1 in *Writing Is Child's Play* for more information about laterality.)

Materials

4″ square cardboard template (cut-off bottoms of milk cartons will work), one per child

manila construction paper—9″ x 12″ sheets

red crayons, one per child

scissors

staplers

STOP sign—large, red paper octagon

tongue depressors (optional), one per child

Preparation

Place the *STOP* sign to the students' right of your teaching area. Like the *GO* sign, the *STOP* sign should be kept up during *itl* lessons.

This activity will go more smoothly if helpers are available to help children make the *STOP* signs.

Activity

Continue the safety discussion started in Lesson 1. Point out the new *STOP* sign, and ask students what the red means on a traffic light.

Demonstrate how to make a *STOP* sign:

• Lay a square template near the edge of a piece of paper. Hold it down firmly with one hand. Draw around it with the other, using a red crayon.

• Color the square red, staying inside the "fence."

• Cut out the red square.

• Draw black lines diagonally across all four corners of each square. Following the black lines, cut off the corners to make an octagonal *STOP* sign shape.

• Fold the rest of the paper into a stick. (You may substitute tongue depressors.)

• Staple the *STOP* sign to the stick.

Have the students make their own *STOP* signs. Helpers can draw the black lines across the corners of the red squares, help students staple the signs to the sticks, and put students' initials on the back.

Check Point

Ask individual children to follow directions with *GO* and *STOP* body parts. For example:

> Put your *STOP* hand on your *GO* knee.
> Put your *GO* foot in back of your *STOP* foot.
> Put your *STOP* thumb on your *STOP* ear.

Take notes so you know which children still need practice. Record individual performance on the Progress Checklist.

Extended Activities

1. Play music with a walking rhythm and have children move with the music. Tell them that when the music stops, they should "freeze" and say "red" or "red light." Stop the music without warning at about twenty-second intervals.

2. Snack time might include slices of red apples, radishes, tomato quarters, cherries, or watermelon chunks.

3. Read several lines of a story very slowly, showing with your finger how the print goes from the *GO* to the *STOP* side of the page and then hops back to the *GO* side again for the next line.

4. Play a game with the *STOP* signs. Tell children you are going to say some things that are true and some that are not true. If what you say is *not* true, they are to raise their signs. If what you say *is* true, they are not to raise the signs. For example:

> Some children are as tall as houses.
> Water is wet.
> Apples are purple.
> The sun shines at night.
> A fire is hot.
> Bicycles have legs.

5. Teach children the second verse of the song introduced in Lesson 1.

Objective To identify three-dimensional objects represented by two-dimensional images.

Understandings The eye must *learn* to see—to make sense out of the nerve impulses that are transferred to the brain from the retina when the eye receives light rays bouncing off an object or a piece of paper. For example, people who are blind from birth and then are given sight through surgery need months of practice before they understand what they see. Understanding what is seen is thus a function of the brain, not of the eye itself. Before reading and writing can be taught, the eye and brain must have had adequate practice in translating two-dimensional images into known, three-dimensional objects. For example, children learn that a flat circle on paper could represent a ball.

Look at the line drawings below. Stare at them for a few moments until they change before your eyes. Your eyes and brain are constantly scanning to make sense of the environment. None of these pictures would have any meaning for your brain unless you had first had experience with the three-dimensional object.

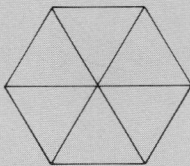

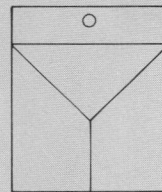

Young children who have not experienced early the joy of discovery through visual stimulation, especially through picture books, will be less eager to participate in beginning writing and reading activities. They will be less motivated to try, because they do not realize that looking can be fun. The purpose of this lesson is to emphasize that *looking* is like solving a puzzle.

Materials

Look-and-Do strips (See *Preparation*.)

Preparation

Make these Look-and-Do strips on strips of tagboard. The size of the strips will vary, depending on whether they are used in small or large groups or for one-to-one teaching. The symbols are simple, black-line drawings. Color a green *GO* spot in the upper-left corner of each strip and a red *STOP* spot in the lower-right corner.

1.

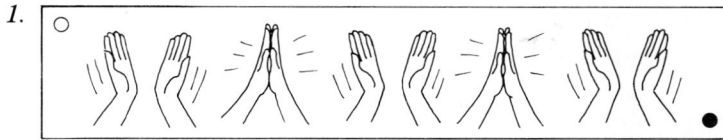

2.

3.

4.

5.

6.

Activity

Look-and-Do Strips 1 and 2 elicit nonverbal actions from students. Put Look-and-Do Strip 1 on a chalkledge or easel where everyone can see it. Point out the *GO* and *STOP* spots on the strips and ask children what each one tells us. Ask one child to "read" the first picture after the *GO* sign by putting his or her hands in the same position. Then point to the second picture and ask the child to do what that picture shows. Ask another child what the lines around the second picture (the "noise" lines) mean. Point out that the little lines tell us the hands are clapping. Continue, asking children to "read" the last three pictures.

Finally, ask another child to do the whole strip again as you move your hand slowly across it; be sure the child stays with you. If you are working with a group, have everyone do it together now. Praise children's achievement—they are *Reading*! Explain that reading means looking at something and then doing what it tells you to do.

Repeat for Look-and-Do Strip 2, having individual children and then the whole group make happy and sad faces.

Look-and-Do Strips 3 and 4 elicit vocal responses. For these strips, touch each picture and ask a child to tell the sound that animal makes. The child is to imitate the sound; don't accept statements such as "he barks." Any dog noise will do (arf, woof, yip). Ask the group to think of a number of different noises the animal makes.

Look-and-Do Strips 5 and 6 elicit real words from children. Without verbal clues, the child is to look at the pictures and name the objects in left-to-right sequence. (Allow ESL students to use their native language; introduce English words as appropriate.)

Check Point

Watch for nonlookers in the group—children who are just imitating others and not really reading the pictures. Call on each of these children to read a strip alone to be sure they understand that this activity requires looking first, then doing.

Record individual performance on the Progress Checklist.

Extended Activities

1. Play a matching game to give children practice responding verbally to pictures. Use any children's card games with duplicate pictures. Displaying pairs of matching and unmatching pictures, review the words *same* and *not the same*.

Turn all the cards facedown. Use only four pairs at first, gradually increasing the number of cards as children's skill grows. The first child to play turns over two cards, naming each one. If they match, the child gets to keep the cards. If they do not, the child returns them to their original places. The second player does the same. Each player tries to remember where the cards are replaced so that he or she can match pairs when they are turned up. The player with the most pairs wins.

2. "Monkey See Monkey Do." Play a record with a strong beat that children can pick up easily. Start the game, moving to the music, but keep changing your activity every group of beats so children will have to watch closely to imitate you, like "real" monkeys. Be sure children are all facing you and not each other. When children have learned the game, choose one of them to be the leader. Work individually with those who have trouble feeling the rhythm so they learn to coordinate movement with the music. Let children lead the game for others to follow.

LESSON 5

Objective To write the initials of one's first and last names.

Understandings Children get pleasure from labeling their own creations. Teaching a large group to write their names correctly, however, is often a difficult and frustrating task. It may be easier to do this after the most frequent alphabet letters have been taught to the group, particularly the most frequently used letters with left curves. *(c, a, d, g, f, s, o, e)*. The *itl Early Writing Program* recommends postponing name writing for most preschool and kindergarten groups, at least until mid-fall. Children who already write their names will probably need individual instruction to prevent them from practicing incorrect letter formation. Children who form letters in incorrect sequences of strokes or directions or who write their names in capital letters need to be corrected before these habits become so ingrained that remediation is difficult. However, learning to make their initials will give children independence in labeling their own drawings and paintings.

Materials

> cardboard/tagboard
> clay—green, red, yellow
> manila construction paper, one sheet per child
> crayons—green, red, yellow, black for each child
> marking pens—green, red, yellow
> mats for rolling clay—foam-backed plastic placemats or other mats, one per child

Preparation

Using colored marking pens, make a cardboard or tagboard sign for each child with her or his first and last initials in the following colors: letter strokes that are made from right to left (toward the *GO* side) should be in green; letter strokes made from left to right (toward the *STOP* side) are red; vertical letter strokes are yellow. *E*, for example, should be made with a vertical yellow line and three horizontal red lines that aim toward the *STOP* side. The letters should be about three inches tall. Use this chart as a color key.

A B C D E

F G H I J K

L M N O P

Q R S T U

V W X Y Z

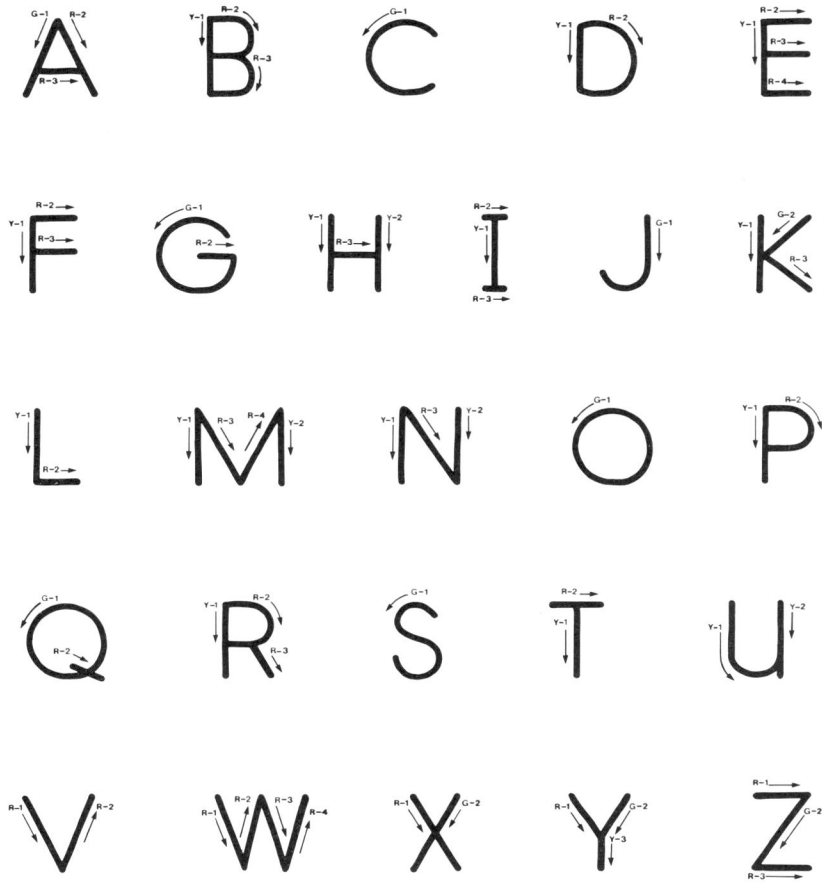

Key
G = Green
R = Red
Y = Yellow

Activity

Say the word *initial* and ask children to repeat it with you. Tell them that this word means the *beginning*. Write a few names on the board and ask a child to point to the beginning of the names on the *GO* side. Explain that the first letter is the *initial* letter. Write pairs of names that begin the same way and that sound the same at the beginning. Be careful not to use examples that begin with the same letter but not the same sound, like *Sharon* and *Sally*.

Give the children the signs you have made with their initials and explain the color key, referring to the *GO* sign and the *STOP* sign in the room. Tell them the yellow lines are the ones that stand up straight.

Show children how to pinch off a piece of clay and roll it into a worm. Then demonstrate how to lay the clay worms, in the correct colors, on top of their initials, matching the colors. Show them how to pinch the worms with their fingertips to make them fit the designs. Tell them to be careful not to mix up the clay colors so they can play the same game another day.

When they have matched their sign correctly, tell them to make their initials out of clay below their sign—not on top of it. Next, take the first sign away and separate the clay pieces so they have nothing to copy. Then ask them to make their initials in the right colors, from memory.

Next, have children write their initials with red, green, and yellow crayons on construction paper. Finally, ask them to use black crayon to make their initials like the printed letters in a book, making the strokes in the correct sequence and going in the proper direction. Just making it look right is not enough. Some children may take several days to complete this task.

Check Point

Check to see that children can make both their initials in the correct stroke sequence with black crayon.

Record individual performance on the Progress Checklist.

Extended Activities

1. Have children make finger-painting posters, repeating their initials to make designs.

2. Make a group mural. When a child can make his or her initials correctly, invite the child to write them on the mural.

2 UNIT

itl
AT THE
GARDEN

hen children have mastered the Unit 1 objectives, they are ready to start writing. Unit 2 teaches children the vertical and horizontal letters— *i*, *t*, and *l*. This unit should take about three weeks with average kindergartners.

Major concepts taught in this unit are:

1. Letters are outline drawings of speech sounds.

2. Letters are made with specific stroke sequences and directions.

3. To make words, letters are written in specific left-to-right order, matching their sound sequence.

4. To make meaningful sentences, words are written in left-to-right order. (A sentence is a complete thought. It makes sense.)

In these lessons, you will begin dictation exercises. Children are to listen to the speech sound you make, repeat the sound aloud themselves, and then write the letter correctly, with no copy in sight, first in the air and then on a writing surface. Avoid using alphabet letter names, and discourage children from doing so. Communication with parents at this point is important so parents don't unknowingly confuse children by using alphabet letter names or by writing capital letters. Sharing *Writing Is Child's Play* with parents may help to clarify this if parents have questions. The parent letter inside the front cover of *my itl book* may be used to give parents information about the *itl Early Writing Program*.

The most effective way to teach letters to young children is to follow this sequence with each letter:

1. AUDITORY First, children listen to the sound.

2. ORAL Merely hearing the sound is not enough. Children must actually repeat the sound. Every child needs to say the sound sometime during the lesson, to imprint the sound in memory. In addition, children should be made aware of the placement of the tongue and lips in making each sound and how it feels to make the sound.

3. TACTILE Every child should feel the letter, tracing its outline in the correct stroke sequence, with the fingers of the dominant hand.

4. KINETIC Every child should imitate you as you write the letter correctly, first in the air and then on a surface. Children need to know from the start that just making letters look right is not enough, but that there is a specific sequence of strokes going in specific directions.

Unless a child has special neurological needs, the tactile and kinetic elements can be combined after the first few letters.

5. *VISUAL* Children need to learn to recognize each letter creature in its two-dimensional form (the outline drawing), and then in its fade-out form (the letter alone).

LESSON 6

Objective To recognize the letter _i_, to say its short-vowel sound, as in _it_, and to write the letter correctly.

Understandings The letter _i_ is pronounced "ih" about 80 percent of the time in English words (Dewey 1970). Therefore, learning this speech sound is far more useful than learning this letter's alphabet name, _eye_. When two related or similar things are taught at the same time (for example, _left_ and _right_, or _b_ and _d_), young learners tend to become confused. Letter names aren't introduced until later in the program.

If children enter school already calling letters by their alphabet names, accept this knowledge casually, saying, "Yes, _eye_ is its last name, just like you have a first name and a last name. We call you by your first name. We're going to learn to call this letter by its first name, _ih_, so we can learn to write and read."

Materials

itl puppet
Audiocassette, Side 1, "_itl inchworm_"
my itl book Activity 1, one per child
black writing crayons, one per child
crayons
newsprint—large, easel-sized sheet for teacher demonstration
black, felt-tipped pen

Preparation

For the activity following the story, tear out the perforated section of _my itl book_ Activity 1 for each child.

You'll be asked to demonstrate most letter-writing activities and drawings for the children. An easel, or easel-sized sheets of newsprint taped to the wall, will be needed for all _itl_ letter-writing activities.

Draw a big _itl_ and a little _itl_ on a sheet of newsprint, making the _i_ black and the rest of the worm yellow. Draw two black _i_'s, one short and one tall, as shown.

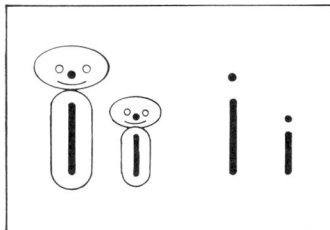

Story

Before telling the story ask students what people mean when they say "ih." Say the sound with an exaggerated facial expression, drawing out the sound on the breath. After several responses, emphasize that the "ih" sound is usually a response to something unpleasant.

Introduce *itl*, displaying the puppet as you either say the verse or play the recording.

itl inchworm

Hello, (*name of child or group*)
I'm an inchworm. My name is *itl*.
Sometimes I'm big, and sometimes I'm little.
(Point to the large and small pictures of *itl*.)
As you can see, my color's yellow.
I'm really quite a friendly fellow.
But when I slither and I squirm,
(Wiggle *itl*.)
People yell out, "ih, (exaggerate sound) a worm!"
That makes me nervous. So I hide,
(Hide *itl* behind your back.)
And all my yellow goes inside.
All you can see is my nose so black,
And a long, long stripe. It, too, is black. (Point to the
letter *i* on the sheet of newsprint.)
I know another tricky trick.
I stand up tall and straight, so quick.
(Show *itl* standing up straight.)
I hide in lots of skinny places.
No one knows just where my face is.
You can find me if you look,
Right inside of any book.
When you find me, big or little,
Say my name out loud, it's ———.
(Wait for children to say *itl*.)

Activity

Ask: "What sound do people make when they see *itl*?" When children respond, say "ih" together several times and then ask individual children to make the sound. Watch to see that children smile as they say *ih*. If there's no smile, the sound will be *eh*. Demonstrate how to feel the muscles of your cheeks pull back when you smile and say *ih*. Correct children who add a second sound (*ih-uh* or *ick*).

Distribute the tear-out section of *my itl book* Activity 1 and black crayons. Explain to children that they are going to draw their own *itl*. Demonstrate how to hold the crayon correctly. Then tell children to write their initials on the *GO* side at the top of their paper.

Demonstrate the steps in drawing *itl* and have children copy the steps to complete their drawings:

On newsprint, with a black, felt-tipped pen, draw *itl*'s stripe from top to bottom and then make a dot for his nose.

Point out the space between the line and the dot and tell children that the dot is not a circle or a ball. To reinforce the stroke sequence, lead children in writing the letter in the air: with your pen still in writing position, use your whole arm to make the vertical top-to-bottom stroke. Then add the dot.

Draw *itl*'s outline around the letter, as shown.

Draw his eyes and mouth.

Write *i* in a talking balloon as you make the sound.

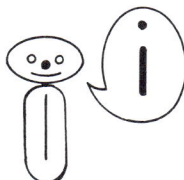

Have children write three more of *itl*'s letter below the drawing, each time saying the sound. Encourage children to color *itl* yellow and green.

Check Point

While children are finishing their drawings of *itl* ask each child to make *itl*'s speech sound and to draw the letter in the air.

Record individual performance on the Progress Checklist.

Extended Activities

1. Distribute *my itl books* and crayons. Have children write their initials on the cover of their book. Then have them turn to page 1. Tell them to trace *itl*'s letter with their finger and then to write the letter in the talking balloon as they say his sound. Then have them color *itl*.

2. Distribute Activity Sheet 3, crayons, and scissors. Have children color and cut out *itl*. Then help them attach the cutout to a folded strip of construction paper or a wooden stick, to make a stick puppet. The stick puppets may be used by the children to copy *itl*'s actions as you re-read the verse.

3. Tell children that *itl* hides in words in books. Then have them look for *itl*'s letter in printed material. Remind them that sometimes *itl* is big and sometimes he's little. Have them look for different-sized *i*'s. If some children have trouble with this activity, remind them to look for *itl*'s tiny dot. As children find *itl*, guide them by placing their index finger under the letter and asking them to say the sound, *ih*.

Cut out lowercase *i*'s in a variety of sizes from magazines and newspapers and mount the letters for display. If children notice that the printed letters look different from the letter on *itl*, explain that that's the way the letter is printed in books but that it is *written* the way they are writing *itl*'s letter.

4. Explain that *itl* is an inchworm. Show children how long an inch is on a ruler. Show them how to measure items such as books.

5. Read *Inch by Inch*, by Leo Lionni (New York: Astor-Honor, 1960), for story time. Tell children to watch for inchworms like *itl*. They look like small caterpillars without fuzzy coats. They have legs only in the front and back.

6. Teach children to do the inchworm walk. Have them bend over, keeping their knees straight, and place their hands on the floor, close to their feet. They should keep their feet still and walk their hands forward until their bodies are close to the ground. Then they should keep their hands still and walk their feet forward to meet their hands.

7. Teach children the hand sign for *i*.

8. Send home the parent letter on the inside front cover of *my itl book*.

Lesson Planning and Evaluation

Following is a sample Natural Educational Tasks Lesson Planning and Evaluation form. This form is designed to help teachers be sure they have covered all bases. The basic thinking skills developed in this writing program are identified at the top of the page: Sequence, Language, Identicality (a knowledge of sameness), Directionality (especially top-to-bottom and left-to-right), and Equivalence (not identical, but having the same value). The learning modes at the left side cover five *sensory areas* that stimulate different areas of the brain. (See "Developing Thinking Skills" in *Writing Is Child's Play* for more information.)

A blank form that may be duplicated and used to plan activities for each lesson is included with the *itl* blackline masters. All the blanks for each lesson don't need to be filled in; you should, however, be aware of which squares you are regularly not filling. By planning a specific activity for those areas, you will be sure to cover the needs of all children, regardless of their major learning modes or individual brain development and organization.

Lesson Planning and Evaluation Form
for Natural Educational Tasks

	Sequence	Language	Identicality	Directionality	Equivalence
Auditory		listen to *itl* story			
Oral		repeat /i/ sound			say /i/ sound when shown letter *i*
Tactile		say /i/ when someone writes letter *i* on child's back		trace letter *i*	
Kinetic	trace letter *i* in the air draw *itl* letter animal in sequence	feel cheek muscles pull when making /i/ sound	leave space between *itl* stick and dot when writing letter *i*	draw letter *i* from top to bottom, adding dot	write letter *i* when /i/ sound is dictated make hand sign for letter *i* do inchworm walk do cut-and-paste stick puppet activity
Visual			look for letter *i* in printed material		

LESSON 7

Objective To recognize and draw vertical and horizontal lines.

Understandings In writing, some young children hesitate to cross the vertical mid-line of their own body. They have strong lateralization tendencies to keep the right and left parts of their body on those specific sides. This interferes with integration of the brain hemispheres needed for efficient writing and reading. These children are sometimes uncomfortable with the task of making horizontal lines going from one side to the other. Occasionally, for example, we see them crossing the letter *t* in two separate strokes, each from the vertical line out. Other children may turn their paper to make the horizontal task a vertical one. This habit, of course, will slow down learning to write efficiently, as well as the development of the left-to-right movement necessary for reading. Give individual help to children who are crossing the letter in separate strokes or turning their paper.

Materials

itl puppet
crayons—black, green, red for each child
newsprint—one 12″ x 15″ sheet per child, one large, easel-sized sheet
black, felt-tipped pen

Activity

With the children facing you, put on the *itl* puppet. Have *itl* explain the activity.

> Hello, boys and girls.
> Today we're going to work on standing and resting lines.
> Now I'm standing. (Hold *itl* in a vertical position.)
> Now I'm resting. (Hold *itl* in a horizontal position as he says: "Ohhhh, I'm so tired. I've been helping boys and girls all day. This feels so good!")
> (Hold *itl* in a standing position as he asks: "What am I doing now?")
> (Change *itl*'s position several times, having *itl* repeat the question.)

When children are able to identify *itl*'s position readily, give each child a sheet of newsprint and a green, a red, and a black crayon. For *itl* drawing or writing lessons, all children must face the same way. Some teachers have children kneel on the floor and use chair seats for writing surfaces. Some use lap boards. Some, with the help of aides, do this part of the lesson with half of the class at a time. One teacher tips tables so their surface is vertical and children can kneel to write. She uses large clamps to hold the paper in place. (A writing slate has been included with the *itl Early Writing Program*. If such slates are available, these may be substituted for the newsprint.)

See that children's newsprint is placed with a short side at the top. If necessary, point out that two sides are short and two sides are long. Remind children of the *GO* and *STOP* signs at either side of the writing area. Then tell them to pick up their green crayon. Give these directions, pausing for children to respond to each one:

- Point to the *GO* sign with your green crayon.
- Pretend to draw a green circle around it.
- Find the *GO* side of your paper.
- Draw a green circle at the top of your *GO* side.
- Now draw a green line down the *GO* side, all the way to the bottom.
- Put your green crayon down.

- Pick up your red crayon.
- Point to our *STOP* sign.
- Find the *STOP* side of your paper.
- Draw a red line down the *STOP* side, all the way to the bottom.
- Put your red crayon down.

- Pick up your black crayon.
- Draw a standing line on your paper, like mine. (Demonstrate.)
- Now draw a resting line, starting on the *GO* side.
  (Demonstrate.)

Repeat, giving verbal directions: standing, resting, standing, resting, etc. Then tell children to put their initials at the top of their paper, near the *GO* side.

Check Point

Have individual children draw standing (top-to-bottom) and resting (left-to-right) lines in the air or on the chalkboard. Work especially with children who hesitate when making horizontal lines.

Record individual performance on the Progress Checklist.

Extended Activities

1. Play the piano, alternating between marching rhythms and a familiar lullaby. Have children respond to the musical cues by standing straight and marching in place or by lying on the floor. Demonstrate how to march with knees high, touching hands to opposite knees with each step.

2. Have children side-step toward the *GO* and *STOP* sides on a line drawn on the playground or taped to the floor, alternating direction. To side-step, take a step to the side without turning the body; then slide the other foot until the feet are together. Then have them side-step on a line, crossing one leg over the other. Reverse directions.

3. Review the exercises from the Lesson 3 Check Point section, emphasizing placing *GO* body parts on the *STOP* side, then *STOP* parts on the *GO* side.

4. Have a crawling relay race with two teams, half of each team lined up facing the other half about 30 feet apart. Observe which children do not cross-crawl in smooth coordination (left hand, right knee, and vice versa). These children may have skipped the vital infant crawling period. Work with these children individually, helping them relearn the cross-crawl pattern until it becomes automatic. (See "Developing Thinking Skills" in *Writing Is Child's Play.*)

Objective To recognize the letter *t*, to say its speech sound, and to write the letter correctly.

Understandings The speech sound represented by the letter *t* is an unvoiced consonant. It is made only in the mouth. The larynx (voice box) is not vibrated—the sound is not *tee* or *tuh*. This is an easy speech sound to make. Infants make it quite early in development, and it rarely needs remediation.

Early childhood teachers know from experience that each year a number of children begin school with a low level of acquired visual perception (the ability to make sense out of what is seen). The storybook activities in which children make the letter creatures step by step will help build the visual perception needed to distinguish between letters. These directed drawing lessons also help build the eye-hand coordination necessary for writing. Watch for children having problems with coordination; provide opportunity and encouragement to draw at least once a day. The children may spend a month just covering the paper with scribbles, but one day you will see shapes begin to emerge on the paper and then you will notice great leaps forward in their writing ability.

Materials

 itl puppet
Audiocassette, Side 1, *"til turtle"*
Character Cards 1 and 2
my itl book Activity 2, one per child
black writing crayons, one per child
crayons
newsprint—one large, easel-sized sheet
black, felt-tipped pen

Story

Display the character cards as you either tell the story or play the recording.

til turtle
One day when *itl* was resting under a leaf, he heard a soft sound coming toward him: "t-t-t-t." He looked up to see what it was and saw his friend *til* the turtle carefully looking under every bush and rock.

  "What are you looking for, *til*?" he asked.

  "I'm looking for my watch," *til* answered. "I can hear it, but I can't find it."

  itl laughed and said, "Silly tilly! Your watch is hanging around your neck!"

  "Oh, now I remember," said *til*. "I put it there so I would be sure to be on time for the talent contest next Tuesday at two o'clock."

  "A talent contest!" *itl* said. "Will you wear a ribbon across your tummy with your name on it?"

45

til pointed to her stomach. "I don't need a ribbon," she said. "I already have a tattoo with my initial."

"What is your special talent, *til*?" asked *itl*.

"I don't know yet," *til* answered. "But everybody is good at something. So I'll figure out what it is."

"I sure hope you win, *til*," said *itl*.

"So do I!" said *til*. "Why don't you come along, *itl*? It might be a lot of fun."

And so *itl* and *til* started off together to try to discover *til*'s special talent.

Activity

Tell children: "Put the tip of your tongue at the top of your mouth behind your front teeth. (Pause.) Take a breath. (Pause.) Now, force the air out until it makes your tongue let go. Put your hand in front of your mouth and feel the little burst of air come out. That's the noise *til* was making."

Have children make the /t/ sound several times. Then ask individual children to make the sound.

Facing in the same direction as the children, write the letter *t* in the air, describing the strokes: "Draw a standing line from top to bottom and then a resting line right through the standing line, from *GO* to *STOP*."

Repeat several times, having children write the letter in the air and say the sequence with you.

Give each child a tear-out section from *my itl book* Activity 2 and a black crayon. Demonstrate how to hold the crayon correctly. Then tell children to use their crayon to write their initials on the *GO* side at the top of their paper.

Draw *til* turtle on a large sheet of newsprint as you lead children in completing their drawing:

Trace the standing line on *til*'s tummy from top to bottom. Then trace the resting line from the *GO* side to the *STOP* side.

Touch the *STOP* side of your resting line. Go up and around, like this, to make *til*'s shell.

Give *til* a neck and a head, like this.

Draw a leg on the *GO* side. Put claws on the end of her foot. Draw another leg on the *STOP* side.

Draw two back legs, one on the *GO* side and then one on the *STOP* side.

Draw her watch and then draw a talking balloon on the *STOP* side.

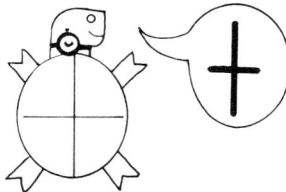

Ask children what sound *til* heard when she couldn't find her watch. Then draw the letter in the balloon.

Tell children to write three more of *til*'s letter below the drawing, saying the sound as they write. Then have them color *til*.

Check Point

While children are drawing and coloring, go from child to child. Ask each child to draw *til*'s letter in the air and to tell you the sound.

Record individual performance on the Progress Checklist.

Extended Activities

1. Distribute *my itl books* and crayons. Have children turn to page 2. First tell them to trace *til*'s letter with their finger and then to write the letter in the talking balloon as they say her sound. Then have them color *til*.

2. Distribute Activity Sheet 4, crayons, and scissors. Have children color and cut out *til*. Then help them attach the cutout to a folded strip of construction paper or a wooden stick, to make a stick puppet. The stick puppets may be used to enact the story.

3. Tello game. Have children play Tello with cards 1-4 from the *itl* Tello cards. Each time they turn over a card, have them say the animal's name and sound.

4. Make Look-and-Do strips to give children extra practice. (See Preparation and Activity in Lesson 4 for more information about Look-and-Do strips.)

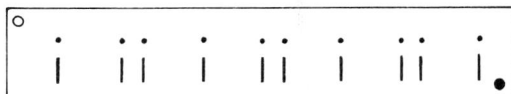

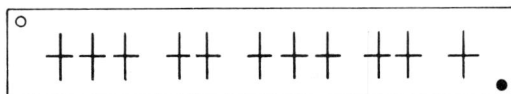

When using the strips, run your finger under the letter from left to right. Show children how to pause on the spaces between the groups of letters when reading the strips.

5. Box of objects. Collect odds and ends that have names beginning with the letter *t;* for example: toothbrush, tack, toy, table. Store the objects in a shoebox labeled with a *t.* Show the objects one at a time and ask children to name them.

6. Teach the hand sign for *t.*

7. Role play. Show children how to pretend to be *itl* and *til.* For *itl,* the child stands straight, feet together; one hand, closed in a fist, is held over the head. For *til,* the child stands straight, feet together, with arms outstretched to the sides. Retell the story about *til* misplacing her watch, letting children take turns being the two characters.

8. Draw the two letters—*i* and *t*—on a child's back with your finger. Ask the child to tell you which letter you made. Do the same on a child's palm (child's eyes should be closed so she or he solves the problem using only the tactile sense). Have pairs of children write the letter *t* on each other's back as they say the /t/ sound together.

9. Give children pages from old magazines and ask them to find and circle *til's* letter.

10. Display Character Cards 1 and 2 one at a time, alternating the sequence, and have children say the speech sounds.

LESSON 9

Objective To blend the sounds /i/ and /t/ into the word *it*.

Understandings Children will be more motivated to learn letters and letter sounds if they see it as a meaningful activity—just as they will learn to count more easily if they do it as a meaningful activity instead of counting by rote. The sooner children start to blend letter sounds into words, the easier it is for them to see a reason to learn letters and letter sounds. The optimum time for teaching any skill is when the areas of the brain controlling that skill are in a growth spurt. Growth in the language centers tapers off at about age five-and-a-half. The easiest pattern to learn to blend is a vowel plus a consonant, as in *it*.

Materials

itl puppet
Character Cards 1 and 2
black writing crayons, one per child
crayons
newsprint—one 12″ x 15″ sheet per child
tagboard letter tags
yarn or string

Preparation

Make tagboard letter tags for the letters *i* and *t* and for the word *it*. Fasten yarn or string to the tags so children can wear them around their neck.

Story

Use the character cards as you present this activity.

itl and til

As *itl* and *til* were on the way to the talent contest, *til* kept thinking about a special talent for the contest. When they passed the pond, *til* wandered off and began writing her initial in the mud at the edge of the pond. Each time she made her initial, she would say the sound, "/t/ . . . /t/ . . . /t/."

When *itl* realized *til* wasn't with him, he started looking for her. As he got near the pond, he slipped in the mud. He got up and looked at his skin. It was muddy all over! Just as *itl* was looking at the mud and saying, "ihhhhhhh," he slipped again. *itl* slid down the mud to the edge of the water and bumped right into *til*, knocking her into the water! (Move *itl* in a downward slide, running into *til* and knocking her over.)

She swam out and laughed. "We made a word. We made *it*."

Replay the story, asking children to take the parts of *itl* and *til*. Hang *i* and *t* cards on the characters. If a slide is available, *itl* can slide down; if not, children can pretend to slide. Encourage the *itl* character to draw out the /i/ sound.

49

Activity

Distribute newsprint and black crayons. Demonstrate how to hold the crayon and then tell children to write their initials in the *GO* corner of their paper. Dictate the word *it*. You might hold up two fingers, one at a time, as you say each sound; be sure to extend the /i/ sound. Ask children which sound they hear first; tell them that the sound they hear first is the one they are to write first. Say the word again slowly and tell children to write *it*.

Ask children what the word *it* means. (It can stand for anything.) Then have children think of something that could be an *it* and draw it on their sheet of newsprint. When the pictures are finished, have children share them. Each artist can hold up his or her picture and tell what it is, for example, "*it* is a truck," "*it* is a monster."

Check Point

As children are working, ask individual children to write *it* on the chalkboard without visual cues.

Record individual performance on the Progress Checklist.

Extended Activities

1. Play *til* tag. Have the child who is *it* wear the *it* sign. When someone is tagged, the tagged player becomes *it*. Children who are on all fours, like *til* turtle, cannot be tagged.

2. Sing a familiar tune, such as "Twinkle, Twinkle, Little Star," using only the /i/ sound instead of the words. This activity helps prepare children for blending vowels and consonants. Ask children if they can sing the same song using only the /t/ sound. Explain that we can't sing with /t/ because it is made only in the mouth. It isn't spoken, so it is not a singing sound; it is a whisper sound.

3. Write, paint, or embroider the letters *i* and *t* on separate beanbags. Put the *t* beanbag on the floor. Have children toss the *i* beanbag toward the *t*, saying and holding the /i/ sound until it lands near the *t*, and then blending the /i/ with the /t/.

4. Spell *it*, first with hand signs and then with body movement, by having two children stand together pretending to be *itl* and *til*. Use the sounds /i/ and /t/, not the letter names, in spelling.

5. Make word cards for several words, including some words that have the word *it* in them, such as *sit, bite*. Display the cards and ask students which ones have the word *it* in them.

LESSON 10

Objective To recognize the letter *l*, to say its speech sound, and to write the letter correctly.

Understandings If some children already have learned this letter by its alphabet name, *el*, simply tell them that *el* is another name for this letter and that today they are learning its reading and writing name /l/. Also be careful not to add a vowel sound to this letter, as in *luh*.

The /l/ speech sound sometimes develops late. Suggestions for helping children who have difficulty are recommended in Check Point.

Materials

itl puppet
Audiocassette, Side 1, *"lit ladybug"*
Character Cards 1-3
my itl book Activity 3, one per child
black writing crayons, one per child
crayons
glue or paste
newsprint—one large, easel-sized sheet
black, felt-tipped pen
scissors

Story

Display the character cards as you either tell the story or play the recording.

lit ladybug

itl and *til* were walking slowly along, trying to think of something special *til* could do for the talent contest. Suddenly they heard a loud noise: "l-l-l-l-l-l-l!" (Make your voice go up and down as you say the sound.)

"What's that?" cried *til*.

"Sounds like a motorcycle to me," said *itl*.

Just then a ladybug zoomed over their heads and landed on a rock nearby.

"Hi, *itl!*" she called.

"Oh, hi, *lit!*" *itl* said. "You used to be so quiet. What happened to you? You sound like a hot rod!"

"Well," *lit* explained, "I got tired of being a plain, quiet ladybug. So I bought some tailpipes!" *lit* pointed to two small pipes sticking out behind her.

itl smiled. "Terrific!" he said. Then he turned to *til*.

"*til*, this is one of my friends. Her name is *lit*—that's short for little."

til told *lit* about the talent contest.

"Oh, may I go, too?" cried *lit*. "I could show off my new, noisy tailpipes."

itl and *til* agreed, so the three friends set off together, *lit* practicing her flying—"l-l-l-l-l"—and *til* winding her watch—"t-t-t-t-t."

Activity

Have children make *lit*'s noisy sound together. Then ask individual children to make the /l/ sound.

Give each child a tear-out section from *my itl book* Activity 3 and a black crayon. Draw *lit* on a large sheet of newsprint as you lead children in completing their drawing:

With a black, felt-tipped pen, trace *lit*'s stripe from top to bottom. Then, holding your pen in writing position, lead children in writing the letter in the air.

Touch the top of *lit*'s stripe and make a circle starting toward the *GO* side, going down and around to the bottom of the stripe, and then around and back to the top of the stripe.

Draw *lit*'s eyes and feelers.

Draw three big round spots on her *GO* side and three more round spots on her *STOP* side.

Draw two tailpipes. Draw them down, across, and up again.

Draw a balloon and then write *lit*'s letter in the balloon.

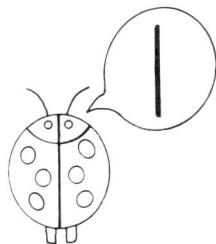

Tell children to write three more of *lit*'s letter below the drawing, saying the sound as they write. Encourage them to color *lit*.

Check Point

While children are finishing their picture, go from child to child, asking each one to make the ladybug's noise. Make a note of children whose mouths are in an /oo/ position; they have not yet acquired the /l/ speech sound. For children whose /l/ sound is not clear, the major problem is often the relaxed mouth, not the tongue position. Have these children look into a mirror and place the tip of their tongue on the roof of their mouth, just behind their teeth (the same place as for /t/). Tell them to keep the tongue there and make a big smiley face. Then ask them to keep smiling and turn on their motor sound (the voice box down in their throat). Tell them to place their fingers on the front of their neck to feel the motor going. Practice a bit, reminding them of the sequence: tongue, smile, motor sound.

When they are making the sound more clearly than before, ask them to name objects that begin with the /l/ sound. These children could make a scrapbook of pictures of objects that have this sound in their name.

Record individual performance on the Progress Checklist.

Extended Activities

1. Distribute *my itl books* and crayons. Have children turn to page 3. First tell them to trace *lit*'s letter with their finger and then to write the letter in the talking balloon as they say her sound. Then have them color *lit*.

2. Distribute Activity Sheet 5, crayons, and scissors. Have children color and cut out *lit*. Then help them attach the cutout to a folded strip of construction paper or a wooden stick, to make a stick puppet. The stick puppets may be used to enact the story.

3. Tello game. Add cards 5 and 6 from the *itl* Tello cards. Remind children to read the pictures aloud when playing Tello. Visual matching alone will not build readiness for writing and reading.

4. Look-and-Do strips. Make Look-and-Do strips with the letters *i*, *t*, and *l* in random patterns. Use these for children who need more practice.

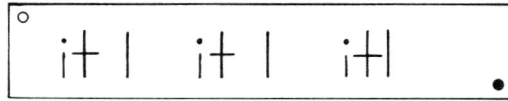

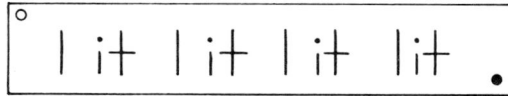

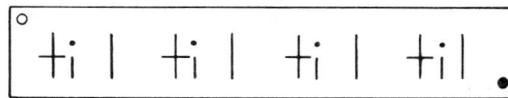

5. Box of objects. Collect objects whose names begin with /l/ (lemon, lollipop, light bulb—flashlight-size for safety). Put these in a box labeled *l* and use them for sound practice and sorting activities with the *i* and *t* objects collected earlier.

6. Teach the *l* hand sign. Always use the right hand for signing. Explain that this sign is the capital *L*—we don't write it that way except for names—and that the /l/ letter looks backward to us because we're in back of it.

7. Have children role play the story. Children can pretend to be *lit* ladybug by standing with their feet together and both arms together above the head. Have other children pretend to be *til* and *itl*. Retell the story as children enact it, or have them dramatize it using their own words.

8. Send home Parent Letter 3.

LESSON 11

Objective To blend the sounds /l/, /i/, and /t/ into words and to write the words from dictation.

Understandings The easiest sounds to blend together are those in the vowel-consonant (VC) pattern. We have already introduced this pattern with the word *it*. Next in difficulty are those in the continuant consonant-vowel (CV) pattern. Continuant consonant sounds are those whose speech sounds can continue until you run out of breath: /f/, /l/, /m/, /n/, /r/, /s/, /v/, and /z/. The most difficult for beginners to blend are those syllables beginning with a consonant whose speech sound is exploded out of the mouth or cut off by the lips or tongue. These "stopper" consonants are *b*, *d*, *g*, *j*, *k*, *p*, and *t*. Therefore, blending /li/ is easier than /ti/; *lit* is easier to blend than *til*; *man* is easier than *pan*; and *fin* is easier than *tin*.

Materials

Character Cards 1-3
black writing crayons, one per child
crayons
newsprint—one 12″ x 15″ sheet per child
strips of 1″ tagboard—one for each left-handed child
toy car

Story

Use Character Cards 1-3 to present this story. Place *lit*'s card in the toy car and put *itl* and *til*'s cards together.

lit, *itl*, and *til*

itl, *til*, and *lit* were on their way to the talent contest. *itl* and *til* were playing tag and yelling *"it"* when they tagged each other. *lit* kept flying around, enjoying the noise of her new motor. As she was flying along the garden path, she noticed a small toy car that she had left in the garden a long time ago. She swooped down and landed right in the driver's seat. The car started moving, and *lit* started driving along, making her soft motor noise, "l-l-l-l-l." Just as *lit* was rounding a curve, she saw *itl* and *til* playing tag right in the middle of the path. They didn't see her coming, and she didn't know where the brake was! Quickly, *lit* felt for the brake. The car came to a stop right in front of *itl* and *til*. All three were making their sounds at once. *lit* was saying, "l-l-l-l-l," *itl* was saying, "ihhhhhhh," and *til* was saying, "t-t-t-t-t."

When *itl* heard the sounds, he said, "We said /l/, /i/, /t/. We made your name!"

Ask for three volunteers to replay the story. Have two children pretend to be *itl* and *til* playing tag. They might hold the character cards to show the word *it* or use body movements to show *itl*'s and *til*'s actions. Have the third child pretend to be *lit*, running downhill and making the /l-l-l/ sound. *lit* stops abruptly before running into *itl* and *til;* then the three characters blend their sounds to say *lit*. Repeat the role play several times with other groups of children.

Activity

Distribute newsprint and black crayons. Tell children to use the crayon to write their initials in the top *GO* corner.

Dictate the word *it*, holding up a finger as you say each sound. Remind children to write the first sound they hear, and then the next sound.

When they've written *it*, show them how to leave a space before they begin their new word: For right-handed students, demonstrate leaving a space two fingers wide between each word. Give left-handed students a strip of tagboard about 1'' wide to hold in their nonwriting hand as a spacer. Hold up three fingers, one at a time, as you slowly dictate /l/ /i/ /t/. Ask children to repeat the sounds back to you slowly, holding up their own three fingers, one at a time, as they make each sound. Finally, ask them to write *lit* on their papers, saying each sound as they write. Show children how to make a period as a *STOP* sign at the end of the sentence. Have them run their fingers under each word and read back what they have written: "*it lit.*"

Ask children what the word *lit* means, besides being the ladybug's name. If children don't make suggestions, ask what these sentences mean:

He *lit* the lamp.
She *lit* the campfire.
The bug *lit* on my head.
The newspaper *lit* on my doorstep.

Have children use the black crayon to illustrate the sentence *it lit*. Tell them to draw the black outlines first (like the lines in a coloring book) and then to color their pictures.

Check Point

While children are drawing, slowly dictate the words *it* and *lit* to individual children, asking them to write what they hear without visual cues. Children who have not yet distinguished between the *GO* side of their bodies and the *STOP* side (left and right, respectively) and those who have not internalized the left-to-right pattern of written English may have trouble learning to write these words. Work individually with them.

Record individual performance on the Progress Checklist.

Extended Activities

1. As an oral language exercise, have children describe their "*it lit*" pictures, telling what is happening in the picture.

2. Have children use cards 1-5 from the *itl* Tello cards to make the words *it lit*.

3. Add the words *it* and *lit* to your Look-and-Do strips. These patterns will help children blend sounds into words.

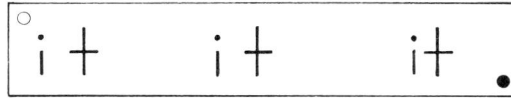

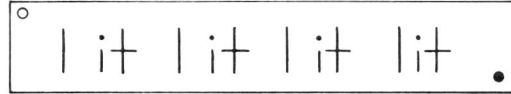

i +   i +   i+ .

| i+ | i+ | i+ | i+ .

4. Have children use magnetic lowercase letters to form the words *it* and *lit* in a metal baking pan as you dictate them.

5. Play "Clap the Chunks." Say a multisyllable word familiar to the children, such as *fan-tas-tic, ham-burg-er, pan-cake;* or proper names, such as *Pa-tri-cia* or *Al-ex-an-der.* Teach children to listen for the syllables (chunks), and then to clap for each one, as they say the word. When the whole group can do it, ask individual children to respond. Reverse the game, saying a word slowly, syllable by syllable, and asking children to say it fast (without clapping).

Objective To blend the sounds *i*, *t*, and *l* into the names *itl*, *lit*, and *til*, and to form the words from dictation.

Understandings Blending sounds into words can be a game, like counting a stack of blocks. In counting blocks, we usually give each one a name, such as *one*, *two*, or *three*. Sometimes it helps to touch each block as we name it. Similarly, when blending words, children should look at or touch each letter and say its reading and talking sound, not its alphabet name. For example, "/l/-/i/-/t/— that word is *lit*." Another word for blending is *sound-spelling*.

Materials

green construction paper—one 6″ x 15″ strip per child
manila construction paper—one 12″ x 15″ sheet per child
cutouts of *itl*, *til*, and *lit*, one of each for each child
glue or paste
scissors

Preparation

From the materials listed above, prepare a diorama for telling the story: Make fringe along one side of a green strip to represent grass; glue the green strip to one edge of a sheet of manila paper. Tuck the three animal cutouts in the grass as shown, without fastening them to the diorama. (The animal cutouts from Activity Sheets 3, 4, and 5 may be used for this activity.)

Story

Present this story using the diorama and cutout characters.

itl, til, and lit play a name game

til was getting tired of playing tag. She told *itl* and *lit* that she wanted to play "Hide in the Grass" instead. At that, *lit* took off and flew up in the air: "l-l-l-l."

   itl said, "That's no fair! Up in the air, you can find us right away! Let's play 'Follow the Leader.' I'm first!"

   Right away, *til* said, "I'm next."

lit said, "I'm last."

(Show the diorama.)

itl said, "That's my name! If we stand like this, we're making my name—*itl!*"

(Run your hand along the grass and ask children to make the animals' special noises in sequence: /i/ /t/ /l/. Do it several times, slowly at first and then faster. Move the cutouts as you continue the story.)

lit said, "Let's do my name." She flew up and over, so she was in front of *itl*.

(Ask children to read the sounds (/l/ /i/ /t/) as you point to them, slowly at first and then faster.)

Then *til* said, "Now it's my turn. Change places with me, *lit*."

(Remove *til* and move *lit* into the end position. Have children read the two sounds /i/ /l/, at first slowly and then faster. Then put *til* in first place and ask children to make her sound very fast, followed by *il*.)

Activity

Tell children that they are going to make a Follow-the-Leader game just like yours. Demonstrate how to cut fringe for grass and how to paste the bottom inch of the grass to the manila sheet.

When they are finished, give children animal cutouts. Show them how to move the animals around in the grass to make the three names. Point out that when they are making an animal's name, that animal is first in line (for example, *l* starts *lit*'s name).

Check Point

Dictate the three names and ask children to make the names, placing the animal cutouts in the grass as they sound out the words. When their animals are in place, tell children to run their fingers under each creature in sequence as they say its sound. Emphasize that reading is a look-and-say game, not a remembering game.

Record individual performance on the Progress Checklist.

Extended Activities

1. To give children practice making words, place an oil drip pan from an auto supply store against a wall and use it for independent group play with magnetic letters. Encourage children to make any words they know.

2. Use rhyming activities to give children practice blending sounds. For example, say an ending syllable, such as *an*, and have children contribute beginning sounds: *ban, can, fan, gan, dan.* Children may know some of these words; however, meaning is not important.

3. Play "Clap the Sounds." This is like "Clap the Chunks" in Lesson 11, except only single sounds in short words are used. Say a three-letter word, such as /m/-/o/-/m/, telling children to clap once for each speech sound. Repeat, saying the word more rapidly. After doing this for several three-letter words, change the game by saying a word rapidly first and then having children say the word slowly, clapping once for each speech sound. The easiest beginning sounds to blend are the continuant consonants that carry on the breath: /f/, /l/, /m/, /n/, /r/, /s/, /v/, and /z/. For example: *fit, lot, met, nob, rip, sad, van, zap.* Endings can be either continuant or stopper consonants.

Objective To review letters and speech sounds for *i*, *t*, and *l*, and to review the words *it*, *lit*, *itl*, and *til*.

Understandings Children at this stage need to know that when speech noises are said quickly in groups, we call them *words*. Words can be nonsense words, just groups of sounds with no meaning, or they can be real words. When we say real words, someone else who speaks our language will understand what we are saying. Some children will write the words in this unit from dictation without obvious effort. But five minutes later they may not remember what they have written. This is strong evidence that writing is easier for young children than reading. The writing tasks stimulate hand, eye, and ear to work together and gradually develop the coordination of the two brain hemispheres necessary for later efficient reading. Reading will grow out of writing; it will happen spontaneously when the brain is ready. (See *Writing Is Child's Play*.)

Materials

itl puppet
Character Cards 1-3
black writing crayons, one per child
Look-and-Do strips
newsprint—one 12″ x 15″ sheet per child

Preparation

Prepare these Look-and-Do strips.

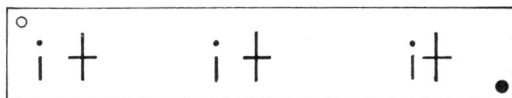

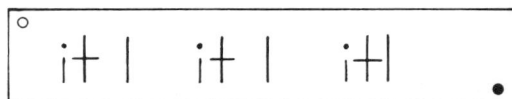

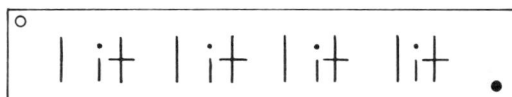

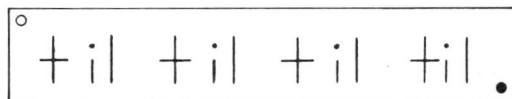

Activity

Give each child a sheet of newsprint and a black crayon. Have all children facing in the same direction.

Demonstrate the following steps, showing children how to fold their paper to make a book:

Lay the sheet of paper flat with the short sides at the top and bottom. Demonstrate picking up the two corners nearest their body and matching those corners to the top corners.

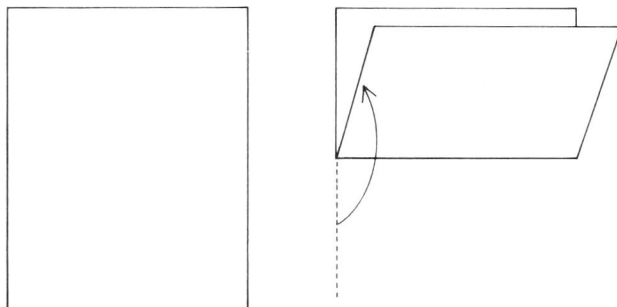

Hold the two sides of the paper with one hand and "iron" the fold with the other hand. (If children pick up the paper to press the fold, explain that the paper might tear.) Turn the folded paper so that the fold is on the *GO* side.

Explain that they have made a book and that pages are always fastened on the *GO* side and open on the *STOP* side. Then have children write their initials in the *GO* corner of their book cover.

Tell children to open their book. Sound out *itl*'s name and have children repeat the sounds slowly as they write the letters on one page. Then repeat for *lit* and *til* having children write each name on a separate page.

Tell children to draw a picture of themselves on the front cover and to draw each letter animal above its name.

Check Point

Ask individual children to read the Look-and-Do strips with the four words: *it, itl, lit,* and *til.* (See Preparation.) Make note of any children still needing review.

Record individual performance on the Progress Checklist.

Extended Activities

1. This would be a good time to invite parents for a party. The children can show off what they have learned, informally or with directed activities. You could serve crackers, each imprinted with one of the three letters in colored, low-sugar cream cheese frosting. Children can demonstrate making the four words with their crackers before eating them. The children can take home their books from this lesson and their Follow-the-Leader diorama from Lesson 12 to practice making the words at home.

2. The sequenced drawings of the first three characters, shown in Lessons 6, 8, and 10, can be enlarged, mounted in manila folders, and used as independent activities, possibly at a learning center.

3. Practice finger-spelling the four words taught, using the sign language for each letter. All children enjoy new coding games. Also, this exercise will strengthen the finger muscles for writing. Finger-spell the words and have children read them; then reverse the activity, saying the sounds and having children finger-spell.

4. Body-spell the words *it, lit, itl, til* and have children decode them; then let individual children do the body-spelling.

3

itl
AT THE
MEADOW

he major concepts of reading and writing the English language have been introduced in the first two units of the *itl Early Writing Program:* letter-sound association, correct stroke sequence, left-to-right progression, words, and sentences.

Unit 3 introduces the letters *j, c, a, d, g, f, s,* and *o.* The letter *j* is a transitional letter that starts with a vertical line, like the letters taught in Unit 2, and ends in a left curve. All of the other letters introduced begin with a left over-curve. In addition, the concept that letters sometimes represent more than one sound is emphasized; two sounds for *s* and the four most frequently used sounds for *o* are taught. Nonsense words are used in some of the dictation exercises to stress listening and sound-sequencing skills.

You may want to introduce the Unit 3 letters and sounds faster than those in Unit 2—two letters a week for average kindergarten groups.

Without very careful instruction, young children may reverse the letters introduced in this unit. The problem is that the curve toward the left is one of the hardest writing strokes to learn to make. When executing that curve, right-handed children cannot see the line being made because their writing hand covers the line. Children are more comfortable when they can see the lines they are making. Also, the first stroke on these letters is a *push* stroke. Push strokes—away from the body—are harder to make than strokes that pull toward the body. Consequently, children may substitute a pull stroke for a push stroke, thereby reversing the letter. Left-handed children have the same problem with letters oriented to the right.

Some writing programs use the "two o'clock" position as a reference for left-curve letters. Children are shown that these letters start at two o'clock on a circle, push up toward twelve o'clock, then around. But two problems arise with this method: The two o'clock position requires the child to estimate where to begin. Also, the child's hand still hides the line being made.

An easier way for young beginners is to start at the top, rather than the side, of a letter and to make left-curve letters in italic form, with flat tops. With the italic form, children can keep their writing hands below the writing line so they can see what they are doing. Most of these letters aim toward the *GO* side with the first stroke. Later, with fluency, children will gradually round these letters. They will rarely reverse them.

c̄ ā d̄ ḡ f̄ s̄ ō

LESSON 14

Objective To recognize the letter *j*, to say its speech sound, and to write the letter correctly.

Understandings The letter *j* is easy to learn to make. Point out to children that *j* looks just like *itl*'s letter but has a curly tail. The problem for beginners is which way to curl the tail. The *GO* sign is the clue. Point out that *jac* is facing toward the *STOP* sign. Therefore, when he jogs, his back leg will bend toward the *GO* side.

In situations where children are learning both Spanish and English or where names begin with *j* (as in José), you can add to the story. For example, the Spanish jack rabbit has been jogging so much that he is out of breath and pants like this (in Spanish words), /h/ /h/ /h/.

Materials

itl puppet
Audiocassette, Side 1, "*jac jack rabbit*"
Character Cards 1, 2, 4
my itl book Activity 4, one per child
black writing crayons, one per child
crayons
newsprint—one large, easel-sized sheet
black, felt-tipped pen

Story

Display the character cards as you either tell the story or play the recording.

jac jack rabbit
itl and *til* were making a sand castle in *itl*'s garden.

lit had flown off to practice some fancy flying stunts. All at once *itl* and *til* heard a new sound: "j-j-j-j-j." Whatever was making that noise was coming closer and closer, because the noise was getting louder and louder.

"Here it comes!" yelled *itl*. "Run!"

A little jack rabbit skidded toward them. He was going so fast he couldn't stop. He slid into their sand castle and knocked it over.

"Are you hurt?" asked *til*.

"No," said the jack rabbit. "The sand is soft. But I ruined your castle. I'm sorry."

"Why do you make that sound?" *itl* asked. "We thought a motorbike was going to run right over us!"

The jack rabbit laughed. "Jack rabbits have to stay in condition, you know. I jump rope and jog every day. It's more fun if I pretend to have a motor.

"My name is *jac*. And I'm really sorry about the sand castle. Maybe I could help you build it up again."

Together, *itl*, *til*, and *jac* rebuilt the càstle while *til* told *jac* about the talent contest. *jac* said he would go along to the contest and do some rope-jumping tricks.

When the castle was done, *til* wrote *jac*'s initial on the side of it.

The talent contest was coming closer and *til* still hadn't decided what to do. "But everyone has a talent," she said to herself. "I'll think of something."

Activity

Ask children to say *jac*'s motor sound, *j-j-j* not *juh*, several times. The speech sound for this letter in English is made by placing the tongue in exactly the same place as for *t*, at the top of the mouth, behind the teeth. Instead of an explosion of air, as in /t/, the tongue is pushed forward on the roof of the mouth. At the same time, the voice box is turned on. Give children these clues—tongue, push, voice.

Facing in the same direction as the children, write the letter *j* in the air, describing the stroke: "Pull down and curve toward the *GO* side. Then add the dot." Repeat several times, asking children to write the letter in the air and describe the stroke along with you.

Distribute the tear-out section of *my itl book* Activity 4 and black crayons. (See the information on animal drawings in the front of this guide.) Demonstrate how to hold the crayon correctly. Then tell children to write their initials on the *GO* side at the top of their papers. Draw *jac* on a large sheet of newsprint as you lead children in completing their drawings:

Draw *jac*'s letter from top to bottom, curling it toward the *GO* side. Then add the dot.

Draw *jac*'s head, ears, body, and legs.

Then add the talking balloon and write the letter in the balloon as you say *jac*'s sound.

Tell children to write three more of *jac*'s letter below the drawing, saying the sound as they write. Then have them color *jac*.

Check Point

While children are drawing, go from child to child asking each one to make the speech sound and to write the letter in the air or on a chalkboard.

If necessary, help children make this sound by having them look into a mirror. Children whose native language is Spanish may say /ch/, the unvoiced speech twin to /j/. Place their fingers on the front of their neck until they can feel the sound "wiggle" inside when they say /j/.

Record individual performance on the Progress Checklist.

Extended Activities

1. Distribute *my itl books* and crayons. Have children turn to page 4, trace *jac*'s letter, and write a *j* in the talking balloon. Then tell them to color *jac*.

2. Distribute Activity Sheet 6, crayons, and scissors. Have children color and cut out *jac*. Then help them attach the cutout to a strip of folded construction paper or a wooden stick, to make a stick puppet. The stick puppets may be used with those made earlier to enact the story.

3. Add the /j/ sound and letter to the activities begun in earlier lessons:

Tello game (See Extended Activities in front of *Lesson Guide*.)
Look-and-Do strips (See Lesson 4.)
Box of objects that begin with the /j/ sound (See Extended Activities in Lesson 8.)
Magnetic letters (See Extended Activities in Lesson 12.)

4. Teach the hand sign for the letter *j*.

5. Have children form the letter *j* with their body, saying the /j/ sound as they make the letter.

6. Encourage children to replay the story about *jac*. Have children pantomime the story as you reread it and then dramatize it using their own words. (See information about dramatic play in the front of the guide.)

7. To suitable music, jog with the children around the playground or room. Make *jac*'s sound while you jog.

8. Begin to teach the children to jump a rope turned by others. This will take a long time and much practice. It is, however, an excellent exercise for helping develop knowledge of the space around the body, which is vital for writing and reading success. Tell children to *listen* and to jump up fast when they hear the rope touch the ground. Show children how to land on their toes with their knees slightly bent to help cushion the shock.

9. Begin to teach the jumping jack exercise for coordination and sequencing. Lead children in doing it very slowly at first, teaching them to jump in the air and clap their hands overhead in a rhythm. When they can do this, add footwork, having them spread their feet apart and clap their hands overhead as they jump. Then have them jump again, simultaneously dropping their arms to their sides and landing with their feet together.

10. Dictate nonsense words to build listening and sound-sequencing skill. For example, say /l/ /i/ /j/ slowly and ask children to repeat the sounds. Explain that /l/ /i/ /j/ is a *nonsense* word and that *nonsense* means that it makes no sense; it might make sense in another language, but *lij* has no meaning in English. Repeat for *ijl, tij, jit.* Dictate the sounds again and have children respond either by standing like the letter animals or with finger-spelling, and then by writing the word. Encourage them to imagine a meaning for the nonsense words, to illustrate the word creatively, and then to share their drawings.

LESSON 15

Objective To recognize the letter *c*, to say its hard sound, as in *music* and *cat*, and to write the letter correctly.

Understandings The letter *c* represents the sound heard at the end of music three times more often than the sound heard in *city* (Dewey 1970). Most words that use the latter sound were originally French words. When practicing this letter and its major sound, don't use words in which *c* is followed by *i*, *e*, or *y*, such as *city, ice, cycle*. (See Appendix B in *Writing Is Child's Play.*)

Materials

itl puppet
Audiocassette, Side 1, "*cat caterpillar*"
Character Cards 1, 2, and 5
my itl book Activity 5, one per child
black writing crayons, one per child
crayons
newsprint—one large, easel-sized sheet
black, felt-tipped pen

Story

Display the character cards as you either tell the story or play the recording.

cat caterpillar

At last the day came for the talent contest. *itl* and *til* set out early in the morning for the meadow where the contest was to be held.

 til didn't say much. She still hadn't decided what her talent was to be. And time was running out. She had to think of something soon.

 As they walked along—slowly, because *til* was busy thinking—they heard a soft cough: "c-c-c-c."

 itl stopped and looked at *til*. "Do you have a cough?" he asked. *til* shook her head. "No, that wasn't me."

 Around the bend in the path they saw a furry green caterpillar. He was bent almost double and was making a soft coughing sound: "c-c-c-c."

 "What's the matter?" cried *itl*. "Can we help?"

 "c-c-c-c. No," said the caterpillar. "I was just combing my fur, and I breathed in a bit of fuzz. It's stuck in my throat and it tickles! c-c-c-c." When his coughing spell was over, the caterpillar explained that he was going to the talent contest.

 "Oh?" said *itl*. "What is your talent?"

 "I'm so pretty I don't need a talent," said the caterpillar. "When the judges see my beautiful green hair all fluffed up like this, I'm sure I'll win." He continued to comb his hair and before long was coughing again: "c-c-c-c."

itl gave him a gentle pat on the back. "We're going to the talent contest too," he said. "We might as well walk together. I'm *itl*. And this is my friend *til*."

"My name is *cat*," the caterpillar told them. It's the first part of my long name, c-c-c-*caterpillar*."

itl and *til* sat down to rest a moment and wait for *cat* to stop coughing. *til* found a little stick and drew a picture of *cat* in the sand, all curled up.

"That looks like the first part of my name," said *cat*, "the part that says c-c-c-c."

til stopped drawing. She closed her eyes for a moment so she could think better. "What, oh what is my talent?" she wondered. "I must be good at something."

Activity

Ask the children to say *cat*'s sound several times. Explain that *cat*'s sound is a "whisper" sound, like /t/: we use the mouth but not the voice when we say it. Then ask individual children to make the /c/ sound.

Facing in the same direction as the children, write the letter *c* in the air, describing each stroke: "A resting line toward the *GO* side, then curve down, around, and up." Repeat several times, asking children to write the letter in the air and describe the strokes along with you.

Distribute the tear-out section of *my itl book* Activity 5 and black crayons. Have children write their initials on the *GO* side at the top of their paper. Demonstrate each step of the drawing on newsprint as you lead children in completing their drawings:

Draw *cat*'s letter toward the *GO* side, down and around, and up again.

Draw the outline around the *c*, *cat*'s face, and fur as shown.

Then add the talking balloon and write the letter in the balloon as you say *cat*'s sound.

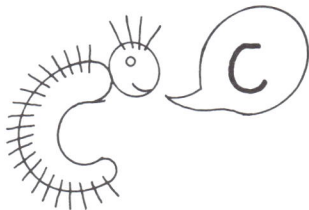

Tell children to write three more of *cat*'s letter below the drawing, saying the sound as they write. Then have them color *cat*.

Check Point

While children are drawing, go from child to child, asking each one to make the new speech sound and to write the letter in the air or on a chalkboard. If necessary, remind children to curl the letter up at the bottom.

Very young children or those with immature speech may substitute /t/ for /c/ (*titty tat* instead of *kitty cat*). Use a mirror to show them how to touch the tip of the tongue to the floor of the mouth. This raises the back of the tongue, closing off the air passage until an explosion of air forces out the /c/ sound.

If children call this letter "see," accept it as another name for the letter. Then tell them that to read and write most words, we need to use the letter's first name, /c/.

Record individual performance on the Progress Checklist.

Extended Activities

1. Distribute *my itl books* and crayons. Have children turn to page 5, trace *cat*'s letter, and write a *c* in the talking balloon. Then tell them to color *cat*.

2. Distribute Activity Sheet 7, crayons, and scissors. Have children color and cut out *cat*. Then help them attach their cutout to a folded strip of construction paper or a wooden stick, to make a stick puppet. The stick puppets may be used with those made earlier to enact the story.

3. Add the /c/ sound and letter to the activities you've already established: Tello game, Look-and-Do strips, box of objects that begin with the /c/ sound, magnetic letters.

4. Teach the hand sign for the letter *c*. Explain that the hand sign *looks* backward to the person making it because when you make hand signs, you are talking to someone facing you.

5. Have children form the letter *c* with their body. Remind them that the opening of the *c* faces toward the *STOP* sign. Tell them to make the /c/ sound as they make the letter.

6. Choose several volunteers to replay the story. You will need a child to play *itl*, one to play *til*, and one to play *cat*. Have children pantomime the story as you reread it, and then dramatize it using their own words.

7. Take a nature walk. Observe any insects you find. Begin a study of insects, pointing out the three body parts (head, thorax, abdomen) and six legs. Tell children that caterpillars take a long sleep and sometimes turn into beautiful moths or butterflies. *itl* is a special kind of caterpillar called an inchworm or a measuring worm because of his funny way of walking. There are no legs on the middle of his tummy. He has six very short legs up front and some extra feet near the tail to help him balance. These back feet are not real legs because they will disappear when he turns into a moth or butterfly. You might follow up the discussion by reading a book, such as *The Very Hungry Caterpillar* by Eric Carle (World Publishing, 1969).

8. Play "Catch Cat." Materials: plastic bleach or water container and a beanbag. Make a catcher by cutting off the bottom of the plastic jug. Draw a *c* on the beanbag. Children toss the beanbag in the air and try to catch it with the plastic catcher. This helps to develop arm muscles for writing and enhances visual tracking and general eye-hand coordination.

9. Send home Parent Letter 4.

LESSON 16

Objective To recognize the letter *a*, to say its short-vowel sound, as in *at*, and to write the letter correctly.

Understandings The letter *a* represents eight different speech sounds in English. The three most common are the sounds for *a* in the words *at*, *about*, and *ate*. The short-vowel sound (*at*) is used seven times more frequently than the long-vowel sound (*ate*). The most useful *a* sound for beginning readers and writers to know is the short-vowel sound. The other sounds for *a* can be taught later. (See "Phonics" in *Writing Is Child's Play*.)

This vowel sound is made with the mouth open. It is one of the "jaw dropper" vowels. The only other vowel taught so far in the *itl Early Writing Program*, the short *i*, belongs to the "smile" group of vowels, those made with a spread of the lips.

Some handwriting manuals recommend teaching this letter in two separate strokes: first the curve, then the "stick." This two-stroke task requires children to estimate where to begin the "stick"—somewhere in the space above the curve—in order to make it fit exactly. Many beginners (late four- and five-, and early six-year-olds) do not have the solid, internalized, left-right knowledge, the ability to estimate space, nor the mature coordination needed to make this two-stroke *a*. Thus their *a*'s are often open at the top, more like the letter *u*.

When their *a*'s don't look right, children often use their common sense to figure out a better way to solve the problem: they begin by making the stick first. This gives them a beginning place to start the curve and eliminates the necessity to estimate, but tends to cause reversals of the letter. They will again apply the "stick-first" solution when learning the letter *d*, which presents the same problem as the *a* made with two strokes. This is where they get into trouble: a reversed *a* can still be decoded, but a reversed *d* becomes a *b* and is obviously incorrect. Children who make their *d*'s with a "stick-first" pattern frequently confuse *d* and *b*.

Teaching children the continuous-line *a*, made without lifting the writing tool, will not only prevent problems with *d* and *b* later on but will also lead directly to the rounded cursive *a* expected in the later primary grades. A second form won't need to be taught. Teaching beginners to make the flat-top form first helps to prevent the open top.

Materials

itl puppet
Audiocassette, Side 1, "*anny ant*"
Character Cards 1, 2, 5, 6

my itl book Activity 6, one per child

black writing crayons, one per child

crayons

newsprint—one large, easel-sized sheet

black, felt-tipped pen

Story

Display the character cards as you either tell the story or play the recording.

anny ant

itl, *til*, and *cat* were walking slowly along the path toward the big rock in the meadow when they heard a sound above them: "a-a-a-a!"

"Look out!" *itl* called. "It's up there!"

They all looked up and saw a leaf floating down like a parachute, with an ant hanging onto it and crying, "a-a-a-a!" A big puff of wind whirled the leaf around and around.

The ant hung on tightly, all the while crying, "a-a-a-a!." Finally the wind stopped, and the ant floated down and made a perfect landing, "a-a-a-a!"

"What's the matter? Were you afraid, coming down like that?" asked *itl*.

"Did you hurt yourself?" asked *til*.

"No, I'm not afraid. And I'm not hurt!" the ant sniffed.

"After all, I am training to be an astronaut. But you just walked over my anthill. Now there will be dust all over inside! I just cleaned it this morning."

"We're sorry," said *itl*. "Maybe we can help you clean it."

"I'll just move these rocks," said *til*.

"Oh, no!" cried the ant. "Don't move the rocks. Those are for my rock-lifting exercises. Astronauts have to be strong, you know."

"Don't expect me to help," sniffed *cat*. "I don't want to get my fuzz dirty before the contest."

itl explained about the talent contest. "Why don't you come along?" he asked the ant. "Rock lifting is certainly a talent."

"Why, maybe I will," said the ant, "as soon as we get this place cleaned up. By the way, my name is *anny*."

"Why, her initial starts just like *cat*'s," thought *til*. "You just close the circle and then make a little stick on the side." She wrote the initial in the sand while she waited for *anny* to get ready to go.

At last *anny* was ready and they all started off together. As they traveled, *cat* kept combing his hair.

"He does look pretty," thought *til*, "but it's not how you look but what you can do that's important in a talent contest."

Activity

Ask the children to say *anny*'s sound several times. Point out that their mouth is about halfway open when they make *anny*'s sound. Then, facing in the same direction as the children, write the letter *a* in the air, describing each stroke: "Over to the *GO* side, down, around, all the way up, and down again." Repeat several times, asking children to write the letter in the air and describe the strokes along with you.

Distribute the tear-out section of *my itl book* Activity 6 and black crayons. Have children write their initials on the *GO* side at the top of their paper. Demonstrate each step of the drawing on newsprint as you lead children in completing their drawings:

Draw *anny*'s letter as you describe the stroke sequence.

Draw *anny*'s body, head, and legs, as shown.

Then add the talking balloon and write the letter in the balloon as you say *anny*'s sound.

Tell children to write three more of *anny*'s letter below their drawing, saying the sound as they write. Then have them color *anny*.

Check Point

While children are drawing, go from child to child, asking each one to make the new speech sound for you and to write the letter in the air or on a chalkboard. Record individual performance on the Progress Checklist.

Extended Activities

1. Distribute *my itl books* and crayons. Have children turn to page 6, trace *anny*'s letter, and write an *a* in the talking balloon. Then tell them to color *anny*.

2. Distribute Activity Sheet 8, crayons, and scissors. Have children color and cut out *anny*. Then help them attach the cutout to a folded strip of construction paper or a wooden stick, to make a stick puppet. The stick puppets may be used with those made earlier to enact the story.

3. Add the /a/ sound and letter to the activities you've already established: Tello game, Look-and-Do strips, magnetic letters.

4. Teach the hand sign for the letter *a*, emphasizing that it resembles the written letter.

You might draw the outline of the letter on children's fists with a nontoxic felt pen: Tell them to close their eyes and feel the /a/ as you trace the *a* shape. Starting on the top knuckle near the thumbnail, go around to the *GO* side, around the palm, up to the top of the thumb and down again.

5. Have children form the letter *a* with their body, saying the /a/ sound as they make the letter.

6. Choose four children at a time to replay the story, first pantomiming it as you reread it and then dramatizing the story using their own words.

7. Give children newsprint and black crayons. Dictate the word *cat* and tell children to write the word sound by sound. Then ask them to illustrate the word in two ways: by drawing a picture of *cat* the caterpillar and a picture of a pet cat or a picture of a large tractor (sometimes called a "cat").

8. Make feely boxes for letter-sound identification. Materials: small round oatmeal boxes, old socks, scissors, tape, colored contact paper, and magnetic letters. Cut off a sock above the heel and stretch the cut-off edge over the open end of the oatmeal box. Tape the cut edge of the sock to the box and wrap the box in brightly colored contact paper. In the container, put plastic or magnetic letters *i, t, l, j, c,* and *a* that have the same shape as the lowercase letters on the *itl* animal characters. Choose a child to reach into the box, feel a letter, and say its sound. Then have the child pull out the letter to see if she or he was correct. Have children play the game in pairs, correcting each other.

9. Find and read a book about ants. Point out the three body parts (head, thorax, abdomen) on Character Card 6, and count the legs.

10. Play a record or tape with a walking rhythm as children crawl in a line, like ants. Give individual help to children who aren't using a smooth, cross-lateral crawling pattern.

Objective To recognize the letter *d*, to say its sound, as in *sad*, and to write the letter correctly.

Understandings A young child, before working with *b* and *d*, has had little opportunity to learn that when an object changes position, it can also change its value and name.

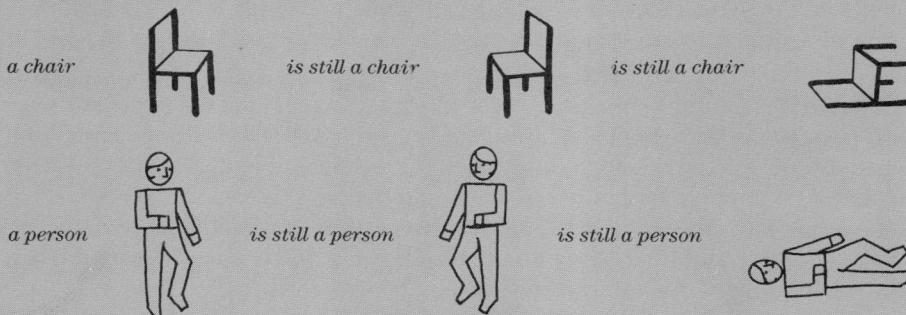

a chair   *is still a chair*   *is still a chair*

a person   *is still a person*   *is still a person*

Therefore it may be very difficult for young children to understand that *b* changes into *d* when it faces the other way. Unless these two letters are very carefully taught, young children will believe there is really no difference and will use the two letters interchangeably in writing and reading. This habit is difficult to break. Since young children are often unable to *see* the difference between these two letters, *kinetic* rather than *visual* methods of instruction should be used.

Also, the letter *d* will be confused with *b* if both these letters are taught close together in time, as in alphabetical order, *a b c d.* Beginning readers and writers need the *d* quite early in alphabet instruction, particularly for word endings (*had, did, and, end*). Since the letter *b* appears only about one-third as often as the letter *d* in written English (Dewey 1970), the *b* can easily be postponed until *d* is familiar. In this program the teaching of *b* is deliberately postponed until most of the other curved letters have been taught.

Preventing children from writing the "stick" first is the most important thing to remember when teaching the letter *d.* Once this habit begins, children must pause after making the stick and decide on which side to draw the curve. This is a difficult decision for children whose knowledge of left-right isn't firmly established. Often, laterality for objects outside one's own body doesn't develop until age eight or later.

Children who make left-curve letters in a stick-first fashion tend to become guessers and sometimes confuse *d* and *b* for years.

As with the letter *a*, the stick-first *d* results from the child's inability to estimate where to begin the second stroke so that it will exactly meet the two ends of the already-made curve. The guesswork and confusion can be avoided if children are taught to make the strokes for the continuous-line *d* over, around, and up. What looks to your eye like an unfinished *d* is not incorrect. This is the original form of the continuous-line *d* designed in the eighth century. The downstroke was added later to facilitate joining letters into words.

When children can trace on a vertical line, they can then be taught to add the last downstroke. Eventually, with fluency, the over curve and the under curve for joining will be added. Children won't need to learn a second system for handwriting. The original form simply gets elaborated as the child matures.

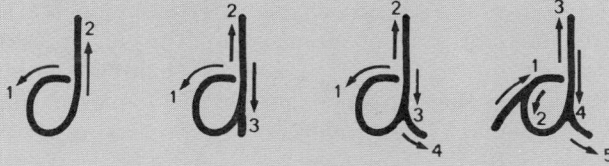

Materials

itl puppet
Audiocassette, Side 1, "dotty dalmatian"
Character Cards 1, 2, 5, 7
my itl book Activity 7, one per child
black writing crayons, one per child
crayons
newsprint—one large, easel-sized sheet
black, felt-tipped pen

Story

Display the character cards as you either tell the story or play the recording.

dotty dalmatian

itl and his friends were still walking along the path to the talent contest when they heard someone singing. The four friends scrambled around a curve to find out who it was. And there they saw the strangest sight: a small dalmatian dog was standing on her head, singing "d-d-d-d-d-d dotty dog."

"What are you doing?" anny asked.

"Doing? Why, I'm singing!" said the dalmatian. "I'm practicing for the talent contest. How many dogs do you know who can sing while standing on their head?"

"That's talent, all right," said cat. "Too bad you're not pretty, like me. You have grass stains all over your ears."

To make up for cat's rudeness, itl politely introduced himself and his friends to the dalmatian. She seemed pleased to meet them and told them her name was dotty—probably because she was covered with dots. Then she sang her song for them one more time: "d-d-d-d-d-d dotty dog."

While she listened, til wrote dotty's initial in the sand. "That looks like the first letter in my name," said dotty, "the one I always sing." She stood on her head again and began to sing.

"My, but she is talented," thought til. "I wouldn't be surprised if she wins the contest. I wonder if I could do that?" til tried to stand on her head, but that pushed her head way back into her shell. Then til rolled over on her back and tried to sing that way, but she nearly strangled on her watchchain.

itl helped *til* to her feet. He asked anxiously, "Are you all right?"

"I think so," gasped *til*. "I don't know what I'm going to do in the contest. But I know I'm not going to try to sing standing on my head or lying on my back!"

Activity

Ask the group to say *dotty*'s sound together. The sound for *d* is made with the mouth and tongue in the same position as for *t*. The only difference is that the larynx is vibrated for /d/. If necessary, show the children their tongue position in a mirror. Let them place their fingers on their throat to feel the difference between these two speech sounds. Discourage children from adding a vowel (the sound is not *dee* or *duh*).

Write the letter *d* in the air, describing each stroke: "Over to the *GO* side, down and around and way up." Repeat several times, having children do it along with you.

Distribute the tear-out section of *my itl book* Activity 7 and black crayons. Have children write their initials on the *GO* side at the top of their paper. Demonstrate each step of the drawing on newsprint as you lead children in completing their drawings:

Draw *dotty*'s letter, describing the stroke sequence.

Add *dotty*'s head, ear, legs, and spots, as shown.

Then add the talking balloon and the letter *d*, saying the sound as you write the letter.

Tell children to write three more of *dotty*'s letter below their drawing, saying the sound as they write. Have children color *dotty*.

Check Point

As children are finishing their drawings, go from child to child asking each one to make the new speech sound and to write the letter.

Record individual performance on the Progress Checklist.

Extended Activities

1. Distribute *my itl books* and crayons. Have children turn to page 7, trace the letter, and write a *d* in the balloon as they make *dotty*'s sound. Then encourage children to color *dotty*.

2. Distribute Activity Sheet 9, crayons, and scissors. Have children color and cut out *dotty.* Then help them attach their cutout to a folded strip of construction paper or a wooden stick, to make a stick puppet. The stick puppets may be used in role playing the story.

3. Add the new sound and letter to the activities you've already established: Tello game, Look-and-Do strips, box of objects that begin with the /d/ sound, feely boxes, magnetic letters.

4. Teach children the hand sign for the letter *d*.

5. Tell children to form *dotty*'s letter with their body, saying her sound as they make the letter. Some children may be able to stand on their head like *dotty* dalmatian, leaning their body against the wall.

6. Choose several children to replay the story, first pantomiming it as you reread it and then dramatizing the story using their own words.

7. Give children newsprint and crayons. Dictate a short sentence, using the sounds already taught: *i, t, l, j, c, a, d.* Have children write a sentence as you make the sounds slowly, holding up a finger for each sound in a word. Show children how to space between words and how to use a period for a stop sign at the end of a sentence. It's important that the sounds be *dictated* and not written for children to copy. (See "Original Composition" in *Writing Is Child's Play.*)

Examples:

dad did it.	*itl* did it.	*jac* did it.
til did it.	*lit* did it.	*cat* did it.

Ask children to illustrate the sentence. Then have them read it back to you.

8. Make doodle balls. Materials (for each doodle ball): old nylon stocking or half of a pair of panty hose, two sheets of newspaper, 9″ square of green paper or cloth, clear plastic sandwich bag, 6″ piece of string.

Gather the newspaper on the fold to make a big "butterfly." Tie the foot of the nylon stocking around the fold.

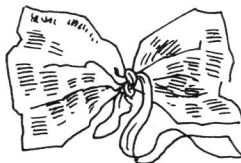

Then crumple the newspaper into a ball. Cover the ball with green paper or cloth; it doesn't need to be fastened.

Tuck the ball into the plastic bag with the stocking hanging out, and tie it firmly with the string.

Tie a large knot at the top of the stocking for a handle.

Show children how to swing the doodle ball in large circles toward the *GO* (left) side. Swing it in a figure-eight pattern. Then change to the other hand and repeat.

Have children swing the doodle balls with their whole arm. Tell them to feel their shoulder muscles moving. Touch their shoulders to show them where their shoulder muscles are.

Doodle balls can be swung in both hands at the same time and swung to music. They build arm control for writing and help strengthen knowledge of left and right sides.

9. Using two drums (large coffee cans with plastic lids will do), sit back to back with a child without touching. (Body contact will give children extra clues; this is an auditory exercise.) Beat out a simple rhythmic pattern:

      d-dd-d-dd   d-d-d-d   dd-dd-dd-dd-dd   ddd-d-ddd-d

Ask the child to say the pattern first, using *dotty*'s sound. Then ask the child to repeat the pattern on the drum. Once they've learned how, children can do this in pairs.

LESSON 18

Objective To recognize the letter *g*, to say its sound, as in *dog*, and to write the letter correctly.

Understandings The letter *g* represents the old-English gutteral speech sound, as in *dog*, three times more often than it represents the soft /j/ sound, as in *cage* (Dewey 1970). The latter (French) sound appears in this letter's alphabet name, so children who already know alphabet names may have difficulty in learning this letter-sound relationship. Simply tell these children they know its last name. Now they need to learn its first name for writing and reading.

When children can write the letters *a* and *j* correctly, it is easy for them to combine these two strokes into the letter *g*. On the other hand, when these two parts of the letter are not shown to them, they often begin at the bottom of the tail, then swoop uphill and around. This habit causes reversals and hinders later fluency.

Materials

itl puppet
Audiocassette, Side 1, "*gus grasshopper*"
Character Cards 1-8
my itl book Activity 8, one per child
black writing crayons, one per child
crayons
newsprint—one large, easel-sized sheet
black, felt-tipped pen

Story

Display the character cards as you either tell the story or play the recording.

gus grasshopper

itl and his friends were getting more and more excited as they got closer to the big rock where the talent contest was to be held.

jac was just rounding the bend, jogging and making his motor sound: "j-j-j-j-j."

Before he could say anything else, they heard a brand new sound: "g-g-g-g-g." (Exaggerate, as if pulling something heavy.)

Soon they came to the creature who was making the sound—a small, green grasshopper wearing a big backpack. He was trying to crawl out of a hole in the ground.

"What's the matter?" *itl* asked. "Are you stuck in there?"

"Not really," said the grasshopper. "But my backpack is so heavy it keeps pulling me back. It's full of health food—granola bars and grape juice. I can't grass *hop* with it. In fact I can't even grass *walk* with it, let alone grass *climb*, which I'm trying to do right now."

itl and his friends helped the grasshopper out of the hole.

"Oh, dear," he groaned. "How can I do my grass hopping at the talent contest with this heavy pack on my back?"

"I've got it!" cried *jac*. "We can help you out. I'm thirsty from all that jogging. Some grape juice would sure taste good!"

The grasshopper—whose name was *gus*—said that would be very helpful, so they all sat down and had a picnic of grape juice and granola bars. While she munched her granola bar, *til* looked at the initial on *gus*'s backpack. She smiled as she thought of the sound *gus* had made when he tried to get out of the hole: "g-g-g-g." "That's the same sound that begins his name—*gus.*" Suddenly *til* laughed out loud. At last she knew what her talent was. Now she was ready for the contest!

Activity

Ask children to make *gus*'s sound. Explain that the speech sound for the letter *g* is made in the mouth the same way as the /c/ sound, except the /g/ sound is voiced by the larynx. Have children place their fingers at the front of their neck and alternate making the sounds for /c/ and /g/ to feel the vibration for /g/.

Write the letter *g* in the air, describing each stroke: "Over to the *GO* side, down and around and up. Close the hole on the side, now slide downhill like in *anny*'s letter. Keep on going with the curl to the *GO* side, like *jac*'s back leg." Tell children to write the letter in the air using whole arm movements, not just wiggling their fingers. The more muscle involvement, the stronger the memory input.

Distribute the tear-out section of *my itl book* Activity 8 and black crayons. Have children write their initials on the *GO* side at the top of their paper. Demonstrate each step in drawing *gus* on newsprint as you lead children in drawing *gus*'s letter and picture:

Draw the letter *g*, describing the stroke sequence and then saying the /g/ sound.

$$g$$

Add *gus*'s head, body, and legs, as shown.

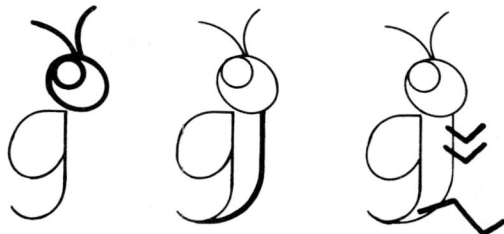

Then add the talking balloon and write the letter *g* in the
balloon as you say *gus*'s sound.

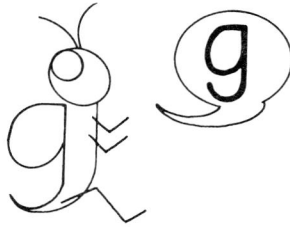

Tell children to write three more of *gus*'s letter below their drawing. Then
have them color *gus*.

Check Point

While children are drawing, go from child to child asking each one to make the new
speech sound for you and to write the letter in the air or on a chalkboard.
Record individual performance on the Progress Checklist.

Extended Activities

1. Distribute *my itl books* and crayons. Have children turn to page 8, trace *gus*'s
letter, and write the letter in the balloon as they say his sound. Have them color
gus.

2. Distribute Activity Sheet 10, crayons, and scissors. Have children color and cut
out *gus*. Then help them attach the cutout to a folded strip of construction paper or
a wooden stick, to make a stick puppet. The stick puppets may be used to enact the
story.

3. Add the new sound and letter to the activities you've already established: Tello
game, Look-and-Do strips, box of objects that begin with the /g/ sound, feely boxes,
magnetic letters.

4. Teach children the hand sign for the letter *g*.

5. Have children form *gus*'s letter with their body, saying his sound as they make
the letter.

6. Replay the story, each time choosing different children to play the parts. Choose
some children who need oral language development for the speaking parts.

7. Distribute newsprint and crayons. Ask children what the word *tag* means; for
example, a chasing game where the person who is *it* tries to touch (or *tag*) the
players; to ticket, as when a policeman will *tag* a speeding driver; a little sign on
something you buy (price *tag*); a little name sign on a gift for someone.

Dictate *tag* slowly, sound by sound, holding up a finger for each letter, and
tell children to write the word. Then ask them to illustrate at least one meaning for

tag. Emphasize that often one word has many meanings. Have children share the pictures for oral language development.

8. Empty and mix the contents of two boxes of objects from your sound collection. Ask children to name and sort the items by their beginning sounds. Try to select partners for this game so a child who is adept at this skill will be matched with one less able.

9. Give children newsprint and crayons. Use these words and phrases for dictation practice:

> *jig dig glad gag*
> *lad dad*

Consonant blends will give young children little trouble if you say them slowly and hold up a finger for each letter.

10. Have a "grasshopper race" in which children hop to a goal. Watch to see which foot each child prefers to use. If it is different from the writing hand, the child may need special help with directionality tasks. (See "Developing Thinking Skills" in *Writing Is Child's Play.*)

LESSON 19

Objective To review the letters and sounds *i, t, l, j, c, a, d, g,* to write words from dictation using these letters, and to read the words.

Understandings At this point, some students will still be at the single-letter stage for dictation. Others will be able to write whole words from dictation. A few will be able to look at the words, say the sounds slowly in sequence, then blend the sounds into meaningful words. When children play tag outside, all children play, no matter how fast they can run. Similarly, children who are still at the single-letter stage should be involved in dictation games. Praise such children when they get any letters right.

Materials

> *itl* puppet
> Audiocassette, Side 1, "*the talent contest*"
> Character Card 9
> black writing crayons, one per child
> crayons
> newsprint—one 12″ x 15″ sheet per child; one large, easel-sized sheet
> black, felt-tipped pen

Story

Display Character Card 9 as you either tell the story or play the recording; have newsprint available for writing *til*'s words.

the talent contest

It was almost two o'clock when *itl, til,* and their new friends arrived at the talent contest. *itl* sat down on the grass with the audience. He wondered what *til* had decided to do for the contest. She wouldn't tell anybody.

Just then the announcer stood up to introduce the contestants.

"Our first contestant," he announced, "is *anny* ant. *anny*'s talent is weight lifting."

anny rolled a rock as big as herself to the center of the stage. Then, to everyone's amazement, that tiny little ant lifted the rock over her head!

itl clapped along with everyone else as *anny* took her bow. The announcer called, "Next is *cat* caterpillar, who will dance." *itl* smiled. *cat* had a talent after all. *itl* clapped as *cat* danced, his beautiful long fur waving back and forth as he swayed to the music. *dotty* was next, and she took everyone by surprise when she stood on her head and sang her song.

One by one, the other contestants had their turn. *lit* did her flying tricks, *jac* his broad jump, and *gus* his grass hopping.

Just then the announcer introduced *til*. She said shyly, "I can write words." She stepped over to a sandy place next to the big rock. With a little stick she began to write carefully in the sand. First she wrote *itl*. Then very carefully she wrote other words in her best handwriting. She wrote (Write these words on the newsprint.):

tag	dig	did
cat	jig	at
lid	jac	dad

When *til* had finished, the audience gave her a standing ovation. That means they stood up and clapped for a long time, while *til* blushed and bowed.

It was no surprise to the audience when the announcer stood up and said, "*til* turtle is the winner." Then he put a crown of flowers on *til*'s head and said, "Congratulations!"

"How did you learn to do that?" asked *anny*.

"Well," she said, "it just sort of happened! I heard the sounds that each of you made, and then I learned to write your initials. So I just put the two things together and figured out how to make words."

Then the group of friends gathered together to finish off *gus*'s grape juice and granola before starting the long trip back home.

Activity

Give children a sheet of newsprint and a black crayon. Demonstrate how to fold the paper into a four-page book. (See Lesson 13.) Show them the front of the book, demonstrating that books open on the *STOP* (right) side. Tell them to write their initials on the *GO* side at the top of their book cover. Select four words that *til* wrote in the story. Dictate each word slowly, giving each sound about one full second and holding up one finger for each sound. Then say the word at normal speed. Encourage children to imitate you, saying each word slowly and holding up a finger for each sound. Next, tell children to write the word at the top of a page. When the four words are completed, tell the children to draw a picture to match each word. When they finish drawing, have children color the four pictures.

Check Point

While the children are working on their books, go from child to child helping children read the words back to you. Tell them to look at each word, run their fingers under it, say the sounds slowly, and then say the word quickly. (Reading is harder than writing; some children may not be ready for this step.)

Record individual performance on the Progress Checklist.

Extended Activities

1. Make books with other words that use the letters that have been taught. For example: *at, cat, dad, did, dig, tag, lid, jac.*

2. Make Look-and-Do strips for the new words.

3. Make letter capes from butcher paper.

       Put one of the letters that has already been taught on the back side of each cape. Masking tape can be used to reinforce the neckline and front edges. Don't put the letters on the front of the capes, or the children wearing them could become confused about left-right orientation of words. Have a child call out one of the words already taught. The children wearing the letters in that word place themselves in the correct order with their backs to the audience.

       The other children read the letters and sound out the word to see that the letters are in the correct order. Observers might be encouraged to finger-spell the words, signing each letter.

4. Make flower crowns. Materials: construction paper, crayons, scissors, and stapler. Give each child a band of construction paper long enough to go around his or her head. Children can either draw flowers on the band or create flowers out of scraps of paper and paste them on, to make them like the crown *til* won at the talent contest. Staple the bands to fit individual head sizes.

5. Choose several volunteers to role play the story. During the enactment, dictate the words for *til* to write. The child who is playing the contest announcer can place a crown on *til*'s head. Encourage the audience to give *til* a standing ovation. Re-enact several times, giving several children an opportunity to play *til*.

6. Play "Hop-Spell." Purchase or make a set of letters imprinted on sponge-rubber squares. (These squares can be cut from plastic placemats.) Use the letters children have learned: *i, t, l, j, c, a, d, g*.

       Have children sit in a circle. Place the letters for a word randomly on the floor within the circle. Then say the word at normal speed, asking a child to repeat the word and then to say it slowly, sound by sound. Have the child hop to the first letter and say its sound, then to the second and third letters, saying the sounds in correct sequence. Finally the child is to say the whole word again. Children in the circle can finger-spell the word while they watch the child in the middle, to see that the word is spelled correctly. Choose another child to play. This game works better in small groups so all children can have a turn.

7. Have a talent contest. Encourage children to show something they can do well. Emphasize that everyone has a talent.

8. Send home Parent Letter 5.

Objective To recognize the letter *f*, to say its sound, and to write the letter correctly.

Understandings Unless young children are taught to write this letter correctly, starting toward the left side, they often get in the habit of first making a *t* and then adding the curl at the top.

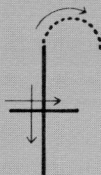

Some children start this letter at the bottom, making the cross-stroke backward, from right to left, because their hand is on the right side at the end of the curl. These habits will have to be unlearned later when children join letters.

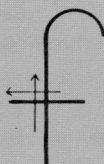

First introducing this letter with the flat-top italic form helps to teach the correct sequence of strokes. The top will round off as fluency develops.

Materials

    itl puppet
    Audiocassette, Side 1, "*fred frog*"
    Character Cards 1, 2, 10
    my itl book Activity 9, one per child
    black writing crayons, one per child
    crayons
    newsprint—one large, easel-sized sheet
    black, felt-tipped pen

Story

Use the character cards as you either tell the story or play the recording.

fred frog

It was a tired but happy group that followed the path through the meadow on the way home from the talent contest. Everyone agreed that *til* deserved to win. Learning to write was a very special talent.

When they reached the pond, *til* said, "Let's stop and cool off for a while. My feet are killing me." With that, she slid into the water and wiggled her toes in the soft bottom of the pond. Then she heard a peculiar soft sound: "f-f-f-f." The others heard it too.

"What's that?" asked *anny*.

itl pointed to a very fat frog who was hopping from rock to rock in the pond.

"Hi!" *anny* called. "You sound like a balloon with a hole in it."

"That's just what I f-f-f-feel like," wheezed the frog. By the way, my name is f-f-f-f-*fred*," he said. "And why does that cute turtle have f-f-f-flowers on her head?"

"Oh, that's *til*," said *itl*. "She just won a talent contest. She can write all our initials—and even words!"

Just then *til* came out of the water. "What is an initial?" *fred* asked her.

"It's the first letter of your name," *til* said. "And your initial stands for the sound you make when you're out of breath: f-f-f-f."

"Oh," said *fred*. "You can write that?"

"Of course," said *til*. She picked up a stick and wrote *fred*'s initial in the wet sand by the pond.

"Say," said *fred*, "Do you suppose you could write that on my shirt?"

gus offered a few drops of grape juice from the container in his backpack. *til* dipped her stick into the juice and carefully made *fred*'s letter on the shirt.

"Thank you, thank you, thank you!" puffed *fred*. "You are just about the f-f-f-finest f-f-f-friend anyone could ever have." With that, he dived into the pond, just to be sure the initial wouldn't wash off in the water. When he came back up, there it was: a beautiful purple initial right in the middle of his green shirt.

Activity

Have children make the /f/ sound several times. Like *t* and *c*, the letter *f* is not voiced. It is a "whisper" sound, made only in the mouth. Tell children to place their top teeth lightly on their lower lip and then blow. The air passing over this partially closed opening makes the /f/ sound. Then have children write the letter in the air using whole arm movements. Repeat several times.

Distribute *my itl book* Activity 9 and black crayons. Have children write their initials in the *GO* side at the top of their paper. Demonstrate each step in drawing *fred*'s letter and picture and have children copy one step at a time:

Trace the letter *f*, pointing out that *fred*'s letter is made toward the *GO* sign and then straight down.

Draw *fred*'s head, body, legs, and arms, as shown.

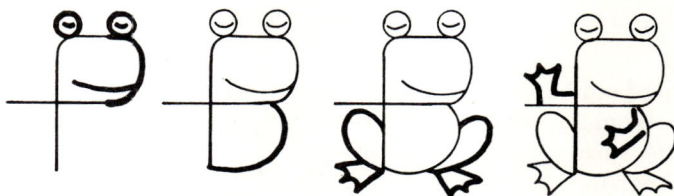

Then draw the talking balloon and write the letter in it as
you make *fred*'s sound.

Tell children to write three more of *fred*'s letter below their drawing, saying the sound as they write. Then have them color *fred*.

Check Point

While children are drawing, go from child to child asking each one to make the new
sound and to write the letter in the air or on a chalkboard. Watch carefully to see
that children are not making the errors mentioned in Understandings.
Record individual performance on the Progress Checklist.

Extended Activities

1. Distribute *my itl books* and crayons. Have children turn to page 9. Tell them to
trace *fred*'s letter and then to write the letter in the balloon as they make his sound.
Then have them color *fred*.

2. Distribute Activity Sheet 11, crayons, and scissors. Have children color and cut
out *fred*. Then help them attach the cutout to a strip of construction paper or a
wooden stick, to make a stick puppet. The stick puppets may be used to reenact
the story.

3. Add the new sound and letter to the activities you've already established: Tello
game, Look-and-Do strips, box of objects that begin with the /f/ sound, feely boxes,
magnetic letters, Hop-Spell game.

4. Teach children the hand sign for the letter *f*.

5. Encourage children to make *fred*'s letter with their body, saying his sound as they make the letter.

6. Choose children to replay the story, first pantomiming their parts as you read the story, then dramatizing it using their own words. You might use a full cast, with all the letter animals in the story, having *itl*, *til*, and *fred* as main characters and having the others in the story simply come in, make their noises, and sit down. Or just use *itl*, *til*, and *fred*.

7. Give children newsprint and crayons. Demonstrate how to fold the newsprint to make a book. (See Lesson 13.) Dictate one word, phrase, or sentence for each page, using the following words:

> *fit*   *fat*   *fig*   *flat*   *flit*   *flag*   *cat*   *dad*
> *fat cat*   *flat flag*   *it fit dad.*
> *fat lad*   *fat dad*

8. Give each child Activity Sheet 12. Tell children you are going to say some words and they are to listen carefully for a certain sound to see if the sound is in the beginning, middle, or end of the word. Explain that if the sound is in the beginning of the word, they are to write the letter in the beginning (first) column; if the sound is in the middle of the word, they should write the letter in the middle column; and if it is at the end of the word, in the last column. Have children repeat each word slowly; this will help them *feel* the letter's position in the word.

Demonstrate the activity by asking children to listen for the /i/ sound in the word *Indian*. When children identify that the /i/ sound is in the beginning, explain that they should write the letter in the first column of the first row. Then have children listen for the /t/ sound in *mitten* and the /t/ sound in *hot*, writing the letters in the appropriate columns.

Continue this lesson over several days, having children identify the position of these sounds in words:

/i/	/t/	/l/
h*i*m	li*tt*le	*l*isten
*i*cky	*t*ag	fa*ll*ing
	ba*t*	unti*l*

/j/	/c/	/a/
*j*ump	*c*at	f*a*t
ed*g*e	i*ck*y	*a*pple
	musi*c*	d*a*d

/d/	/g/	/f/
*d*og	*g*o	*f*ast
hi*d*	tu*g*	i*f*
ba*d*	u*g*ly	ele*ph*ant

LESSON 21

Objective To recognize the letter *s*, to say its sound, as in *cats*, and to write the letter correctly.

Understandings The letter *s* represents its soft sound, as in *soup* and *sat*, about three-fourths of the time it appears in written English. It represents the "buzzy" sound, as in *is*, *as*, *boys*, *girls*, about one-fourth of the time. This lesson teaches the more frequently used sound, as in *cats*.

The sound of *s* is voiced (buzzed) when it follows a vowel or voiced consonant. In *cats* the *s* is not voiced because the /t/ sound preceding it is made only in the mouth. On the other hand, *dogs* has a buzzy *s*, because the preceding /g/ sound is made by vibrating the larynx.

If we told young children that the sound /z/ is usually represented by the letter *z*, we would be giving them incorrect information. Children then would spell like this: *iz*, *az*, *boyz*, *girlz*. The letter *s* represents this speech sound five times more often than the letter *z*.

Children who lisp will need special attention with both of the sounds of *s*.

This letter is one of the most difficult to make. However, children will rarely reverse it if they learn to make the beginning stroke toward the *GO* side, like the other letters in this unit. The flat top helps achieve this goal at first, and will round off with writing fluency.

Materials

itl puppet
Audiocassette, Side 1, "*sissy snake*"
Character Cards 1, 2, 4, 7, 8, 10, 11
my itl book Activity 10, one per child
black writing crayons, one per child
crayons
newsprint—one large, easel-sized sheet
black, felt-tipped pen

Story

Display the character cards as you either tell the story or play the recording.

sissy snake

itl and his friends were just about to leave *fred* frog's pond when they heard this sound: "s-s-s-s-s."

"Oh, oh!" squealed *dotty*. "I think that's a snake sound."

fred laughed. "You're right. It's just *sissy*. She lives here in my pond."

A little green snake slithered out of the water.

sissy smiled. Then she blew out some air with her teeth closed. It made a noise like this: "s-s-s-s-s."

"So that's how she does it," said *itl*. "You just smile, close your teeth, and blow out a little air."

"I can do it, too," said *jac*. "And I can feel the air coming out when I hold my paw in front of my mouth."

fred introduced *sissy* to *itl* and all his friends. *jac* told her about the talent contest.

sissy said, "Oh, I should have been there. I do imitations."

"Oh?" said *jac*. "What kind of imitations can you do?"

"Well," said *sissy*, "I can pretend to be a teakettle with the steam coming out: s-s-s-s-s. And I can be air coming out of a tire: s-s-s-s-s. And I can even be bacon frying in a pan: s-s-s-s-s."

til, of course, was busy showing *sissy* how to write her initial in the sand.

"But *sissy* can't write it herself," said *gus*. "She has no hands."

"Nonsense," said *sissy*. "Who needs hands?" And in no time she had swung her body into the shape of her initial.

Activity

Show children how to close their teeth and blow out air, as *sissy* does. If children are having difficulty making the sound, tell them to close their teeth with their tongue locked behind and make a little smile. Then tell them to blow out a puff of air over the top of their tongue and feel the air come out between their teeth. If you have children who lisp, use a mirror to show them what happens when their tongue peeks out.

Write the letter *s* in the air, describing the strokes: "Start like *cat*'s letter and then go down and around like *jac*'s letter." Repeat several times, asking the children to do it with you.

Distribute *my itl book* Activity 10 and black crayons. Have children write their initials on the *GO* side at the top of their paper. On a sheet of newsprint, demonstrate the steps in drawing *sissy* as children complete the drawing.

Write the letter.

Draw *sissy*'s body and face, as shown.

Then add the talking balloon and write the letter in the balloon as you say *sissy*'s sound.

Tell children to write three more of *sissy*'s letter below their drawing, saying the sound as they write. Then have them color *sissy*.

Check Point

While children are drawing, go from child to child, asking each one to make the new sound and to write the letter in the air or on a chalkboard. This is one of the most difficult sounds for young children to learn to make. It is also one of the most difficult letters to make without reversals. Remind children who are reversing the letter that *sissy* is green so her initial is written starting toward the *GO* side. If some children repeat the first curve instead of making the second curve in the opposite direction, explain that the letter begins like *cat*'s letter and ends like *jac*'s back leg.

Make a list of children who are having difficulty saying or writing the sound so you can give them additional attention with extended activities.

Record individual performance on the Progress Checklist.

Extended Activities

1. Distribute *my itl books* and crayons. Have children turn to page 10, trace *sissy*'s letter, and then write it in the talking balloon as they say her sound. Have them color *sissy.*

2. Distribute Activity Sheet 13, crayons, and scissors. Have children color and cut out *sissy.* Then help them attach the cutouts to folded strips of construction paper or wooden sticks, to make a stick puppet. The puppets may be used to enact the story.

3. Add the /s/ sound and letter to the activities you've already established: Tello game, Look-and-Do strips, box of objects that begin with the /s/ sound, feely boxes, magnetic letters, Hop-Spell game.

4. Teach children the hand sign for the letter *s.*

5. Have children make *sissy*'s letter with their body, saying her sound as they form the letter.

6. Ask for volunteers to replay the story. Have children pantomime the story as you reread it, then dramatize it using their own words.

7. Give children newsprint and crayons. Show them how to fold the newsprint to make a four-page book. Dictate words and have children write the words in their book. Start with three-letter words (*sit, sat, sis, sad, gas*) and then dictate some four-letter words (*cats, sift*). Avoid using words with the buzzy /s/ (*is, his, as*).

8. Have children practice making figure eights with doodle balls, starting toward the *GO* side and then changing the curve. (See Extended Activities in Lesson 17.)

9. Have children who are having difficulty making the /s/ sound say the sound in front of a mirror. Show them how to make it so that their tongue doesn't peek out. Ask these children to collect pictures of objects whose names begin with the /s/ sound, to mount them on a poster, and then to share them with the class.

10. With your finger, slowly write two- and three-letter words on children's backs or on the palms of their hands and ask them to decode the words.

11. Dictate these nonsense words and encourage children to imagine what the words might mean:

tig faf glic sig dit

LESSON 22

Objective To make the /s/ sound, as in *is*, and to distinguish it from the /s/ sound in *cats*.

Understandings This sound is made identically to the /s/ taught in Lesson 21, except the larynx is vibrated. The letter *s* represents this sound in English five times more often than the letter *z*.

Materials

itl puppet

Character Cards 1-8, 10, 11

black writing crayons, one per child

crayons

newsprint—one 12″ x 15″ sheet per child

strips of 1″ tagboard—one for each left-handed child

Story

Display the character cards as you tell the story.

sissy's new sound

itl, *til*, and their friends decided to spend several days with *fred* and *sissy*. One morning they were all swimming together in the pond when *til* heard a new sound. She stretched her neck out of her shell and said, "Listen! I hear something buzzing. Is that a rattlesnake?"

The others listened, too. They heard "z-z-z-z-z." They couldn't figure out what was making the sound.

Suddenly *sissy* burst out laughing. "Do you mean this sound: z-z-z-z-z? That's me! I forgot my towel. And I'm shivering from the cold water. When I shiver, that's the sound I make. z-z-z-z-z."

"Ah, now you can't do your imitations," said *cat* sadly. "Oh, yes I can!" said *sissy*. "But I do different ones. You heard my summer act. Here's my winter one."

As they listened, *sissy* went through all of her cold-weather imitations: an alarm clock, "z-z-z-z-z"; a honey bee, "z-z-z-z-z"; and even a zipper, "z-z-z-z-z." Everyone laughed at *sissy*'s new act.

"Well, no matter what sound you make, your initial stays the same," *til* said, as she wrote it in the sand.

"That's right," said *sissy*, and she formed her initial with her body and said "z-z-z-z-z."

itl shook his head. It would be hard to leave these new friends.

But since they all needed water to live, he couldn't invite them to come with him.

"Well, maybe we can stay here just a few more days," he thought. And that's what they did.

96

Activity

Display Character Cards 1-8 and 10. Point to the cards at random, asking children to say the sound for each one. Display Character Card 11, explaining that children know two sounds for *sissy*. Tell them to make both sounds when you point to *sissy*, /s/ and /z/. Repeat the sound drill including Character Card 11.

Ask children to say *til*'s sound. Then ask them if *til*'s sound is a word. Tell children the difference between a sound and a word. (A word is a group of sounds that means something.)

Explain that when we talk to people we say words in a sentence. For example, the word *cat* tells us one thing. *Black cat* tells something more about the cat. *"My cat is black"* is a whole idea. It tells who owns the cat and the color of the cat. It makes sense.

Say *"is black cat my"* and ask children if those words make sense. Emphasize that these words are not a sentence but just a group of words—they don't make sense.

Give children newsprint and black crayons. Tell children you are going to say a sentence for them to write. Dictate one of the sentences below, saying the sounds slowly and raising a finger for each sound in a word. Point out that it's important to leave space between words so the words will be easier to read. Have right-handed children use two fingers of their left hand to help determine space between words; have left-handed children use a 1″ strip of tagboard to measure the space. Don't expect capitals at the beginning of sentences yet or children may start to use them randomly whenever they write. Remind children to use a period as a *STOP* sign.

> *til* tags sis.
> it is *jac*.
> it is sad.
> cats sit.

Ask children to illustrate their sentence and then to color it.

Check Point

As children draw and color, go from child to child and ask each one to read what he or she has written. Help them run their fingers under each letter from left to right, saying each sound as they go.

Record individual performance on the Progress Checklist.

Extended Activities

1. Give children newsprint and black crayons. Repeat the sentence-writing activity, dictating other suggested sentences or make up your own sentences using the sounds taught.

Add these words and sentences to your dictation exercises:

is	*scat cat.*
flags	*it sat.*
tags	*dad is sad.*
as	
lids	

2. Choose volunteers to dramatize the story using their own words. Use a beach towel as a prop for *sissy*.

3. Draw a large talking balloon and put a nonsense sentence in it. Ask children to decode it and imagine what it means and who might say it. Example: *dil a goj tic*. Dictate a nonsense sentence for children to illustrate.

LESSON 23

Objective To recognize the letter *o*, to say its short-vowel sound, as in *on*, and to write the letter correctly.

Understandings This letter represents many different speech sounds in English. Most of them are made with the lips in the round *o* position. The lips gradually form smaller and smaller *o*'s as you pronounce these words: *on, off, go, to, good.*

Only the major short-vowel sound, as in *on*, is introduced in this lesson. The letter *o* represents this sound, *ah*, three times more often than it represents the sound heard in its alphabet name, *oh* (Dewey 1970). The first sound is a much more useful tool for beginners. (See "Phonics" in *Writing Is Child's Play*.)

The second sound (*off*) is pronounced identically with the first sound (*on*) by some American-English speakers. This language characteristic is dialectic, primarily heard in western Massachusetts, eastern Pennsylvania, central Colorado, and the Pacific Northwest. The majority of American speakers, however, do distinguish between these two vowel sounds. Listen to yourself say *on-off*. If you can't *hear* the difference, try to feel or see the difference. Look in a mirror. Does your mouth shrink a bit on *off*? Try it with *hot-dog*. Do you say d(ah)g or d(aw)g? The latter pronunciation is more common. While young children don't need to learn these fine details at this time, teachers should be aware of them.

Materials

    itl puppet
    Audiocassette, Side 1, "*olly octopus*"
    Character Cards 1, 2, 7, 12
    my itl book Activity 11, one per child
    black writing crayons, one per child
    crayons
    newsprint—one large, easel-sized sheet
    black, felt-tipped pen

Story

Display the character cards as you either tell the story or play the recording.

olly octopus

On their way home, *itl* and his friends came to another pond. This one was full of seawater that had been trapped at high tide. While *itl* and his friends rested, they heard a noise, going up like this—(*raise your voice with each "ah"*) "ah-ah-ah-ah-ah-h-h-h-h"—and then down like this—(*lower your voice as you say the sounds*) "ah-ah-ah-ah-ah-h-h-h-h!" It seemed to be coming from that pond.

"That sure is good singing," said *dotty*. "Whoever it is sings even better than I do. But probably *not* standing on its head like me," she added. They walked to the edge of the pond to see who it was. There they found a small octopus.

"What are you doing here?" asked *itl*. "I never expected to see an octopus near the meadow."

"I came in with the ocean tide," explained the octopus. "But I forgot to go out with it. I'm lonely, so I sing to keep myself company: ah-ah-ah-ah-ah-h-h-h-h!"

"You should have been in the talent contest!" said *dotty*. "You might have won."

"Talent contest?" asked the octopus. "What's that?" *itl* explained about the contest and how *til* had won. Then he introduced all of his friends to the octopus. The octopus said his name was *olly*.

til wrote *olly*'s initial in the wet sand by the pond.

When they left *olly*, he thanked them for stopping. "Please come and see me again," he said. "I really get lonesome here, with no one to talk to."

Activity

Have children say *olly*'s sound several times. Then sing a familiar tune, such as "Twinkle, Twinkle, Little Star," substituting *olly*'s sound /ah/ for the words.

Demonstrate writing the letter *o* in the air, starting with a flat top aimed at the *GO* side. Repeat several times, having children do it with you. Then write *olly*'s letter in the air, singing the sound at the same time.

Distribute *my itl book* Activity 11 and black crayons. Have children write their initials on the *GO* side at the top of their paper. Demonstrate each step of the drawing on newsprint as you lead children in completing their drawings.

Trace *olly*'s letter.

Draw *olly*'s face and arms, as shown.

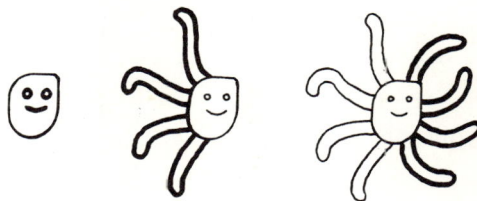

Add the talking balloon, writing the letter *o* in the balloon as you say the /ah/ sound.

Have children write three more of *olly*'s letter below the picture, saying the sound as they write each letter. Then have them color *olly*.

Check Point

While children are drawing, go from child to child asking each child to make the new sound and to write the letter. Watch carefully to see that the letter *o* is made correctly. It must begin with a flat stroke toward the left at the top, then go around, down, and up again.

If children begin at the bottom or circle toward the right, they will need to learn the letter over again when they are expected to join it to other letters later on. This will be difficult if the letter has been made incorrectly for two or more years. It is much easier to insist that children make it correctly in the first place before a bad habit has been established.

Record individual performance on the Progress Checklist.

Extended Activities

1. Distribute *my itl books* and crayons. Have children turn to page 11, trace *olly*'s letter, and then write it in the balloon as they say his sound. Then have them color *olly*.

2. Distribute Activity Sheet 14, crayons, and scissors. Have children color and cut out *olly*. Then help them attach the cutouts to a strip of folded construction paper or a wooden stick, to make a stick puppet. The puppets may be used to enact the story.

3. Add the new sound and letter to activities you've already established: Tello game, Look-and-Do strips, feely boxes, magnetic letters, Hop-Spell game.

4. Teach the hand sign for the letter *o*.

5. Ask children to form *olly*'s letter with their bodies, saying his sound as they make the letter.

6. Choose several children at a time to replay the story. Have children pantomime their parts as you reread the story, and then dramatize the story using their own words.

7. Give children newsprint and crayons. Show them how to fold the newsprint to make a four-page book. Dictate the following *ah* words and have children write the words and then illustrate them: *on, dot, got, lot.*

8. Play "Ghosts." For writing practice, give each child in the group an individual writing slate. Write a letter on the chalkboard and ask children to look at it for about two full seconds. Then, erase the letter—the *ghost* disappears. Ask children to write the ghost letter they saw. Watch to see that letter formation is correct. This game works best with small groups. When children can play this game with single letters, try it with two- and three-letter words that have been introduced.

9. Play "Pass the Beanbag." Materials: eleven green beanbags. Draw the letters *i t l j c a d g f s o* on separate beanbags. Have children sit in straight lines with the *GO* sign on their left side. Have children pass several beanbags at a time while you play music that has a strong beat. When you stop the music at random intervals, tell children to "freeze." Each child left holding a beanbag tells its sound and holds the beanbag in the dominant hand as she or he writes the letter in the air.

As a variation, use letter beanbags to build words. Dictate two- and three-letter words and have children arrange the beanbags to show the words.

10. Tell children to read your lips. Then position your mouth to say the /i/ (*itl*), /a/ (*anny*), and /o/ (*olly*) sound without making any noise. Have children guess which sound you are making and describe the difference in your mouth position as you make each sound: /i/ is a wide smile, /a/ is a half-open mouth, and /o/ is a wide-open mouth. Choose a child to be leader of this game as the other children guess the sounds.

LESSON 24

Objective To make the /o/ sound, as in *off*, and to distinguish it from the /o/ sound in *on*.

Understandings Children will be unable to write independently unless they know sound-symbol relationships for all the sounds of their own spoken language. If the *aw* speech sound is not used in your geographical area, you may want to skip this lesson. If people in your particular region say "ahrange" or "awrange," "sah" or "saw," "dahg" or "dawg," they are using both sounds (*ah* and *aw*) for the letter *o*.

Materials

itl puppet
Activity Sheet 14, one copy
Character Cards 1, 7, 8, 12
black writing crayons, one per child
crayons
mirror
newsprint—one 12″ x 15″ sheet per child

Preparation

Using the picture of *olly* on Activity Sheet 14, prepare a green-colored octopus stick puppet to use as *orville* in the story. Save the puppet for use in Lesson 25.

Story

Display the character cards and stick puppet as you tell the story.

olly and orville

itl and his friends had just left *olly* octopus. They walked around to the other side of the tidewater pond. There they heard someone singing up and down like *olly*, but it didn't sound quite the same. It went, "Aw-aw-aw-aw-aw-aw," and down again, "Aw-aw-aw-aw-aw-aw."

"Could that be *olly*, over here?" asked *gus*.

"It sure doesn't sound like *olly*," said *dotty*. "But there he is—way over there at the edge of the pond. How did he get here so fast?"

All of the friends hurried over to see the octopus.

"Hi, *olly*!" said *itl*. "What's wrong? Your voice sounds different. Do you have a sore throat?"

"I beg your pardon," said the octopus. "My name isn't *olly*. My name is *orville*, but I'm looking for my brother, *olly*."

itl realized then that this was a different octopus. This one was a little bit smaller than *olly* and his coloring was a little bit different. This one was kind of green. *itl* gave *orville* careful instructions about swimming straight across the pond to the other side. Then *itl* and his friends ran along the shore back to where they had left *olly.* They kept calling his name. When they got there, *olly* was nowhere in sight. Then they heard a gurgle from deep in the water. *olly* was resting on some soft sand on the bottom of the tidewater pond.

When he finally heard them, he popped out of the water and started to sing his song, "Ah-ah-ah-ah-ah-ah-ah-ah." At that moment, *orville* poked his head out of the water and sang, "Aw-aw-aw-aw-aw-aw-aw-aw."

The two fellows stared at each other. Then they laughed and started talking at the same time. *orville* had been swept in with the tide just like *olly.* He was waiting for the new tide to come in so he could get back into the ocean too. They were so glad to have found each other that they opened their mouths and sang together like this: "Ah-aw-ah-aw-ah-aw-ah-aw."

til, as usual, was making letters in the sand trying to figure it all out.

"*sissy*'s letter makes two sounds. Now *olly*'s initial is the same as *orville*'s, round like a circle," *til* said. "You hear *olly*'s sound in the word *dot,* but *orville*'s in the word *dog.*"

itl said to all his friends, "They have the same initial. But the important thing is, now they have each other. They won't be lonesome any more."

Activity

Say *orville*'s sound (aw) and have children repeat the sound several times. Then say *olly*'s sound (ah) together. Point out that the mouth is bigger when you say *olly*'s sound than when you say *orville*'s sound. Pass a mirror around so children can see the difference. Say both sounds several times, alternating them as *olly* and *orville* did in the story.

Give children newsprint and black crayons. Demonstrate how to fold their papers to make a book. Remind children that a book opens on the *STOP* (right) side. Tell them to write their initials on the *GO* side of the cover.

Dictate these words with *orville*'s sound and have children write one word on each page of their book:

> *dogs*
> *soft*
> *logs*
> *off* (Explain that this word has two of *fred*'s letters on the end, but we only
>   make one /f/ sound.)

Tell children to draw a picture to illustrate each word. Then have them color their drawings.

Check Point

While children are drawing and coloring, go from child to child, asking each one to make the two sounds for the letter and then to write the letter.

Record individual performance on the Progress Checklist.

Extended Activities

1. Give children newsprint and crayons. Ask children to draw a picture of *olly* and *orville.* Remind them that *olly*'s mouth is larger to make the louder sound.

2. Play Hop-Spell with the letters and sounds taught so far. Be sure to include words that show both sounds for *s* and *o.*

3. Give children newsprint and black crayons. Dictate sentences for children to write:

> *dog is lost.*
> *fat cat is soft.*

4. Use plastic photo cubes to make a set of alphabet blocks. Each block holds five different letters. Use the blocks for drill in the letters and sounds already taught.

5. Use Character Cards 1-8, and 10-12 in drill activities. Display the characters in random order, asking students to say the sounds as you point to the cards. For *s* and *o* have children say both sounds taught for each letter. (/s/ /z/ and /ah/ /aw/)

6. Send home Parent Letter 6.

Objective To discriminate the four speech sounds for the letter *o* (*on, off, go, to*).

Understandings Young children cannot write independently with only twenty-six sounds, one for each letter. They need to know some way to represent in writing all the sounds they make when they talk. The various vowel sounds for the letter *o* are the easiest of the vowels for young children to discriminate, because when making these four speech sounds the mouth is always in the same round shape. The variance is only in the size of the opening.

Of the five name sounds for the five major vowel letters (*a, e, i, o, u*), *o* is the most frequent in English (Dewey 1970). Thus, it is the first long-vowel sound introduced.

Materials

itl puppet
Activity Sheet 15, one copy per child
Character Cards 1, 2, 5, 8, 12
crayons
stick puppet from Lesson 24

Story

Display the character cards as you tell the story. Use the stick puppet from Lesson 24 for *orville* octopus.

olly and orville's rock group
itl and his friends were getting ready to leave the octopus boys, *olly* and *orville*, and head for home.

"I hate to leave," said *til*. "I could stay here all day and listen to them sing together. Sing for us one more time, *olly* and *orville*."

The two octopus singers climbed up on a rock and began to sing again.

"They're singing on a rock," said *gus*. "They must be a rock group."

olly started to sing first. He went up, "Ah-ah-ah-ah-ah-ah-ah-ah." Then *orville* made his voice go down, "Aw-aw-aw-aw-aw-aw-aw-aw."

Then *olly* made his mouth smaller. He sounded like this: "Oh-oh-oh-oh-oh-oh-oh-oh."

Then *orville* made his mouth even smaller. He looked like he wanted to be kissed. He sang, "Oo-oo-oo-oo-oo-oo-oo-oo."

olly told everyone that there were two more octopus brothers back home in the ocean. He said little brother *obie* sings the /oh/ sound, and their baby brother *oopsie*, sings /oo/ all the time.

"It's very confusing," said *cat*. "How can one letter stand for so many sounds?"

til smiled and said, "The better to make words with, my dear." And in the sand *til* wrote words with all of *olly* and *orville*'s sounds. But she used the same letter for all four sounds.

She wrote: *dot, dog, go, to.*

She read the words to the other friends.

"Look!," said *gus*. "Watch *til*'s mouth when she makes *olly*'s and *orville*'s special singing sounds. Her mouth is always round in a circle, like the octopus boys. But the circle keeps getting smaller and smaller, like this: "Ah-aw-oh-oo."

The friends all did it together, "Ah-aw-oh-oo. Ah-aw-oh-oo." They looked so silly that *olly* and *orville* laughed until they both fell into the water.

"We must go now," said *itl*. "We need to get home before dark so we won't get lost. Goodbye, *olly*. Goodbye, *orville*. Thanks for the concert."

And again they headed back to *itl*'s garden.

Activity

Have children practice making the four sounds /ah/, /aw/, /oh/, /oo/. Start with /ah/ and show them that their mouth gets smaller for each sound.

Distribute Activity Sheet 15 and crayons. Tell children that these are the four octopus brothers. Have them draw a wide-open mouth on *olly*, a middle-sized mouth on *orville*, a small mouth on *obie*, and a tiny mouth on *oopsie*. Dictate the following words one at a time and tell children to write each word under the octopus that makes the same sound they hear in the word: *to, hot, go, dog.* Remind children to compare the size of their mouth when they say each word.

Tell children to color the octopus brothers. *olly* is gold. *orville* is green. *obie* is orange. *oopsie* is blue.

Check Point

While children are coloring, go from child to child, asking each one to make the four sounds and to write the letter.

Record individual performance on the Progress Checklist.

Extended Activities

1. Look for the letter *o* in words, pointing out its various sounds. For example:

in the children's names (John, Bob, Cory, Joan, Jo, Lois)
in signs around school, in book titles

Read the words very slowly, sound by sound, asking children to listen carefully and tell you which of the octopus sounds they hear in the word.

2. Have a "Hunt for *to*" game. Let children look through library books printed in large type to see how many *to* words they can find.

3. Use the character cards for sound drill. Have children make all the sounds for *o* when you point to *olly* octopus: /ah/ /aw/ /oh/ /oo/.

4. All of the letters of some children's names have probably been introduced by now. For example, *Todd, Jill.* Check to see that children are writing their name correctly.

5. Have children do jumping jacks. Children clap their hands overhead at the same time as they jump and spread their feet apart. Then they jump, pulling their feet together and dropping their arms to the side at the same time. Lead children in doing this very slowly at first.

UNIT 4
itl AT THE FARM

his unit introduces the letters *e, u, r, n, h, m, p, b.* Each of these letter symbols begins with a stroke toward the right or with a vertical, top-to-bottom stroke followed by a right curve. In addition, the numerals 1-5, whose orientation is toward the right side, and the digraphs *qu* and *ng* are included in this unit.

The activities in Units 1-3 may have developed children's hand coordination to the point where they are ready to write with pencils. If so, remember that young children don't have the arm and finger strength to make dark lines with hard lead. The lead in standard school pencils is usually too hard for beginners. They need to grip these pencils with all their strength to make lines that are dark enough to see. This is exhausting work. Short pencils with extra soft, dark lead are best for young children; regular-length pencils can be cut in half. A soft, plastic, three-sided gripper will help children learn the three-finger grasp. (A sample pencil and gripper of this type are included with the *itl Early Writing Program* materials.) Children should be told that they will probably make mistakes. Instead of erasing, they should be encouraged to draw a line through the mistake and write the letter or word again.

LESSON 26

Objective To recognize the letter *e*, to say its sound, as in *edge*, and to write the letter correctly.

Understandings The letter *e* helps children make the transition from writing left-curve to writing right-curve letters. To write *e*, they start toward the right side and then change direction and make the familiar left curve—over, around, down, and up.

The most common sound for the letter *e* is the short-vowel /e/, as in *edge;* thus, it is taught first. This sound is used three times as often as the alphabet name sound for *e*, as in *eat*.

This sound for *e* is sometimes confused with both the short sound for *i*, as in *it*, and the short sound for *a*, as in *at*. It is not quite the "smile" sound made when saying *it*, nor the "jaw dropper" sound made when saying *at*. This sound is halfway between /i/ and /a/—the mouth is slightly open but still relaxed.

In some areas of the United States, the short /i/ and short /e/ are not distinguished, so the words *pin* and *pen* or *tin* and *ten* sound the same. For young children this dialect becomes a spelling handicap. If children cannot *hear* the difference between the /i/ and /e/, they can be shown how to *feel* the difference: by placing their hands on their cheeks, they can feel the cheek muscles contract when they say *in* and relax when they say *edge*. Saying *in* and then *ten* also demonstrates the difference. Children from Mexican Spanish-speaking homes will use the /eh/ sound naturally. On the other hand, children from South American or Caribbean Spanish-speaking homes may need special help with this sound because it isn't in their language repertoire.

Materials

itl puppet
Activity Sheet 16, one copy per child
Audiocassette, Side 1, "*ed elephant*"
Character Cards 1, 2, 3, 5, 6, 13
my itl book Activity 12, one per child
black writing crayons, one per child
crayons
newsprint—one large, easel-sized sheet
black, felt-tipped pen

Story

Display the character cards as you either tell the story or play the recording.

ed elephant
itl and his friends said good-bye to *olly*, *sissy*, and *fred* and then started for home. Before they'd gone very far, they heard someone softly crying: "eh-e-e-e-e-e-e-eh."

"What's that?" whispered *anny*.

They went into the woods, following the sound: "eh-e-e-e-e-e-e-e-eh." The ladybug, *lit*, flew ahead. "Here it is," she called. "You won't believe what I found."

"You're right," said *cat*, the caterpillar, when they got there. "I don't believe it. A baby elephant in our woods! How did it get here?"

The baby elephant stopped crying. "I ran away from the zoo. And now I'm lost." He stood up.

"What a long nose you have!" laughed *cat*.

"I know," said the elephant. "That's why I ran away. I keep tripping on my trunk. Everybody laughs at me. But now I'm lost. And I want to go home."

"We'll help you find the zoo," said *itl*. "Come with us."

"My name is e-e-e-e-e-e-e-*ed*," the little elephant said.

"Your initial looks sort of like a balloon blowing in the wind!" *til* said. She wrote the letter in the dirt for *ed* to see.

"Wow!" said *ed*. "Is that my initial? I wish I could write like that!"

til looked at him thoughtfully. "With your long trunk you ought to be very good at writing."

"Do you really think so?" asked *ed*. "You mean my long trunk is finally good for something?"

As they walked toward home, *til* said, "Look, why don't you come home with us? On the way, I'll show you how to write letters."

"Then tomorrow I'll take you back to the zoo," *itl* said.

And so the group moved on together with *til* and *ed* writing letters and the others making the sounds.

Activity

Distribute Activity Sheet 16 and black crayons. Demonstrate how to hold the crayon correctly. Then tell children to put their initials in the *GO* corner at the top of their paper. Explain that they are going to draw some lines before they write *ed*'s letter. Have children place their crayon on the neck of the balloon closest to their initials and trace the outline for the balloon starting on the dot and going up toward the *STOP* side, around and down the string, and up again. Repeat for the other two balloons. Then show children how to trace the spiral lines on the bottom, starting in the center, then going around and around, each circle getting larger than the last one. Have them make another spiral, starting at the last dot on the sheet. Have children set the sheets aside.

Ask children how *itl* and his friends knew *ed* elephant needed help. When they respond, repeat *ed*'s cry for help several times together, prolonging the /e/ sound.

Draw a large *e* on newsprint, describing each stroke: "Toward the *STOP* side; change direction and go over, around, down, and up."

Then ask children to write the letter in the air with you, making the sound at the same time. Repeat several times.

Distribute the tear-out section of *my itl book* Activity 12 and black crayons. Have children write their initials on the *GO* side at the top of their paper. Demonstrate the steps in drawing *ed* on a large sheet of newsprint as children complete their drawing.

Draw *ed*'s letter, adding his head, body, legs, tail, and blanket as shown.

Add the talking balloon and write *ed*'s letter in it as you say the /e/ sound.

Tell children to write three more of *ed*'s letter below their drawing, saying the sound as they write. Then have them color *ed*.

Check Point

While children are drawing, go from child to child asking each one to make the new sound and to draw *ed*'s letter.

Record individual performance on the Progress Checklist.

Extended Activities

1. Distribute *my itl books* and crayons. Have children turn to page 12. Tell them to trace the letter and to write an *e* in the balloon as they make *ed*'s sound. Then have children color *ed*.

2. Give each child a copy of Activity Sheet 17, crayons, and scissors. Have children color and cut out *ed*. Then help them attach the cutout to a folded strip of construction paper or a wooden stick, to make a stick puppet. The stick puppets may be used to enact the story.

3. Add the /e/ sound and letter to the activities you've already established: Tello game, Look-and-Do strips, feely boxes, magnetic letters.

4. Teach the hand sign for the letter *e*.

5. Encourage children to form *ed*'s letter with their body, saying his sound as they make the letter.

6. Choose volunteers to replay the story of *ed* elephant. Have them pantomime their parts as you retell the story, or dramatize it using their own words.

7. Play Hop-Spell, using the letter *e* in words; for example: *let, ed, led, test.* (See Extended Activities in Lesson 19.)

8. Use doodle balls for practicing whole-arm movements (See Extended Activities in Lesson 17.)

9. Play the "Chair Game" to help children discriminate between the four short-vowel sounds that have been introduced:

Tell children to sit *in* their chairs all the way, with their back touching the back of the chairs. Then have them sit on the *edge* of their chairs by sliding forward. Repeat, telling them to sit *in* or on the *edge* several times. Then repeat, just saying the sounds /i/ and /e/. Tell children to watch your face carefully as you say the words without making a sound. (/i/ is a wider smile.)

Go back to making sounds, reminding children who had difficulty reading your lips to watch your face and mouth for clues.

When children can distinguish the two sounds, add /a/, having children stand *at* (beside) their chairs when you make this sound. Then add /o/ to the game, having children place one foot *on* their chairs when they hear this sound. Exaggerate your mouth position as you make the sounds; you might want to practice in front of a mirror to make sure children will be able to distinguish the sounds from the position of your mouth.

Choose children to take your place as leader of the game, explaining that they must pronounce the words and sounds very clearly.

10. Make a "Pin the Tail on *ed*" game. Draw a picture of *ed* on a large piece of heavyweight paper. Make tails for the children to use. Sometimes young children are insecure using a blindfold. Instead, place a large bag that rests on the shoulders over the child's head so that the child cannot see the picture of *ed*, but has enough light to walk toward it safely. Draw a happy face on the bag for fun. Making tails for *ed* could be coordinated with a lesson on braiding with thick, soft yarn.

11. Send home Parent Letter 7.

Objective To recognize the numbers 1 to 5, to tell their values, and to write the numerals correctly.

Understandings When young children demonstrate, through manipulative activities such as block play, that they understand basic math concepts such as one-to-one correspondence and equivalence (two short blocks are the same height as one tall block), they are ready to begin to record this knowledge through written numerals.

However, one of the problems in making numerals is that, like letters, they are oriented both toward the left side and the right side. Teaching *2, 3, 4,* and *5*—numerals that are oriented toward the right—at the same time you are teaching letters that are oriented toward the left (*c, a, d*) may cause confusion in young children. They may not understand why their reversals are incorrect.

Numerals are much easier to learn than letters. First, there are less than half as many to learn. Second, their number values are constant until children are ready to learn place-value. (The numeral *1* on the left changes its value from 1 to 10 in the numeral *11.*) Fortunately, the first curved numerals to be learned (*2, 3, 4, 5*) all start in the same direction, toward the right, so we do not need to invent a new sequence, as with letters.

At this point in the *itl Early Writing Program,* children have learned to make left-curve letters. Learning to make numerals 1-5 will help children make the transition toward the right-curve letters introduced in this unit.

Materials

    itl puppet
    Activity Sheet 18, one copy per child
    Character Cards 1, 2, 5, 7, 12
    newsprint—one large, easel-sized sheet
    paper, one sheet per child
    black, felt-tipped pen
    soft-lead pencils, one per child

Preparation

Draw a picture of *dotty* on a large sheet of newsprint, positioning the dots in the same places as on Activity Sheet 18.

Story

Display the drawing of *dotty* on an easel. As the numerals are described in the story, draw the numerals over the dots, as shown.

$$1\ 2\ 3\ 4\ 5$$

dotty's numbers

At last *itl* and his friends were back home. It had been a long day with many adventures. *ed* elephant was going to spend the night. *itl* had promised to take *ed* back to the zoo in the morning.

cat, dotty, itl, til, and *ed* were resting. *til* had already shown *ed* how to make all their initials in the sand. *ed* was learning fast. He held a stick in his long trunk and made letters in the sand.

til was staring at *dotty*'s dots. "Look, *itl*," she said. "You can use *dotty*'s dots for counting. There's one on her tail, two up here, then three, four, and five. I wish I knew how to make the numerals for those numbers."

"I'll show you, *til*," said *itl*. He made a little hole in the sand. "That's like the one dot on *dotty*'s tail," he said. "You just start on that dot and make a straight line. That's a one." (Demonstrate on the newsprint drawing.)

"That's easy," said *til*. "It's just like *lit*'s initial—a long, straight, standing line."

Then *itl* said, "See these two dots up near her leg? If you want to learn to make a two, you must make a curvy line from one dot to the other. Always start on the dot at the top. (Demonstrate.) Now make a resting line aiming toward her back."

All the animals made a two in the sand.

"I can do it!" squealed *ed*. "Won't the other elephants at the zoo be surprised!"

"Now we'll make a three," said *itl*. "See these three dots? You start the three just like the two. Then, instead of a resting line, you make another curve." (Demonstrate.)

"It looks a little bit like two of me," said *cat*, "only my initial curls the other way."

"Four is easy," said *itl*. "See these four dots? Start at the top on the *GO* side. Make a standing line down to the dot underneath. Make a resting line over to the dot on the *STOP* side. Lift your stick and place it on the other dot at the top. Make a long standing line. Make it go right through the dot." (Demonstrate.)

til laughed. "It looks like four is standing on one leg!"

All the animals made a four.

"This numeral is the hardest," said *itl*. "Watch very carefully and I'll show you how to make a five using these five dots. Start it just like the four, in the top *GO* corner. Start down, like four with a standing line, only this is just a little short line. (Demonstrate.) Now start over to the *STOP* side and make a fat curve. Curl it up at the end like *jac*'s back leg. Hit all three dots."

"What's that other dot for?" asked *til*.

"That's how you finish it," said *itl*. "You put the top on last. Go back to the beginning dot and make a resting line over to the other dot. And there's a five."

"Why can't we make the top line first?" asked *til*. "Wouldn't that be faster?"

"Sure, it's faster," answered *itl*. "But when you do it that way, you go so fast you make your corners round and then it looks like *sissy*'s letter." (Demonstrate by drawing a numeral that looks like an *s*.)

"I'm worn out from all this learning," said *ed*. "Let's go to bed."

Activity

Write the numerals in the air one at a time, making large strokes and describing the strokes. Repeat each numeral at least once:

- Start the one at the top and make a long, straight standing line.
- Start the two at the top and make a curvy line toward the *STOP* side. Then make a resting line toward the *STOP* side.
- Start the *three* just like the *two*. Make two curves toward the *STOP* side.
- Start the four at the top on the *GO* side. Make a short standing line and then a resting line toward the *STOP* side. Then make a long standing line.
- Start the five at the top on the *GO* side. Make a short standing line and then a fat curve toward the *STOP* side. Curl it up at the end like *jac*'s back leg. Go back to the beginning and draw a resting line toward the *STOP* side.

Remove the newsprint illustration and give each child a copy of Activity Sheet 18 and a soft lead pencil. Have children draw the numerals on *dotty*'s dots.

Check Point

When children have finished writing the numerals, have them put their activity sheets aside. Give each child a sheet of plain white paper. Dictate the number names in mixed order and have children write the numerals without the dots. If children reverse numerals, draw a red line down the right side of the paper to remind them that these numerals curve toward the *STOP* side and ask them to write the numerals again.

Record individual performance on the Progress Checklist.

Extended Activities

1. Practice writing numerals with finger paints.

2. Have children stand in rows with the *GO* side on their left side, and the *STOP* side on their right. Call out numbers 1-5 in mixed order and ask children to write these numerals in the air. Remind children that these numerals curve towards the *STOP* side.

3. Write the numerals on children's backs with your finger and have them identify the numerals.

4. Teach children to play dominoes using dot patterns up to five. Materials: domino game.

5. Give each child a sheet of paper and a black crayon. Demonstrate how to fold the paper into a four-page book. (See Lesson 13.) Then tell children to number the pages 1-4. Have children draw one item on page 1, two on page 2, three on page 3, and four on page 4.

6. If children can point to the *GO* and *STOP* sides without hesitation when asked to do so, start using the word *left*. An association that may be helpful in teaching this word is explaining that when children leave something behind they have *left* it, and when you move away from the *GO* side, you have *left* it. Tell children that you are going to begin to call the *GO* side the *left* side.

Play Simon Says, using the words *left* and *STOP*. The words *left* and *right* should be introduced separately; suggestions for teaching the word *right* are in Lesson 31, Extended Activities.

Objective To place letters correctly on wide-lined paper.

To recognize the color words *red, yellow, blue, orange, green, purple, brown,* and *black*.

Understandings When children have the control to use pencils, they are usually ready for lined paper. The lines on standard first-grade lined paper are too narrow for beginners. Start with line spacing at least three-fourths inch high for single-space letters, and one-and-a-half inches high for the tall letters already introduced (*l, d, t,* and *f*).

Some children in your group may not be ready for lined paper or for beginning to learn color words. On the other hand, some children who are not sure where to place letters on a blank field feel more comfortable with lines. If your entire group seems exceptionally immature or if you are working with a prekindergarten group, you may want to postpone this lesson until all the letters are introduced.

This lesson may be taught over several days.

Materials

Activity Sheets 19, 20, and 21, one copy of each per child

crayons, one of each color named in the objective per child

soft-lead pencils, one per child

Preparation

Make a sample copy of Activity Sheet 19, coloring *itl*'s house the colors marked on the activity sheet. Display it during the activity as a model.

Activity

Give each child a copy of Activity Sheet 19 and crayons of each color. Explain that this is a picture of *itl*'s house and that the words on the sheet are the names of colors. One color at a time, tell children which color to use and have them outline each area of the house in the color listed. When all areas are outlined, ask children to color each area the same color as the outlines. Tell children to color lightly so their hands don't get so tired.

Give each child a copy of Activity Sheet 20 and pencils. One at a time, have children write each letter in the air with you, holding their pencils correctly as they do it, and then have them trace the letter on their paper. Point out that the letters in the middle line are all tall—they go up to the point of the roof—and that the letters on the bottom line fall into the basement.

Check Point

Give each child a copy of Activity Sheet 21. One letter at a time, dictate the letters *i, c, a, e, o, s, l, f, d, t, j, g* by their major speech sounds and have children write them on the lines.

Record individual performance on the Progress Checklist.

Children who have trouble with this exercise should be given additional practice activities. If a child needs help with specific sounds, use the character cards to assist memory. If a child has trouble forming letters, writing the letters in the air and tracing large letters on an easel or chalkboard may be helpful.

Extended Activities

1. Play "Color Skip." Materials: Cardboard box; green, red, and yellow blocks or balls of paper; tagboard; black marker; white string. Prepare a feely box and place colored blocks or balls of paper (one green, one red, one yellow) inside the box. Give each child a color word—*red, green,* or *yellow* written on tagboard in large, black lowercase letters—on a soft white string to hang around his or her neck. Have the children stand in a circle. Ask one child to sit in the center of the circle with the feely box. Tell the child to reach in and pull out one object. Ask the other children to watch and then to name the color of the object. Children who are wearing the corresponding tagboard color word step to the outside of the circle and skip around and back to their place, and the rest of the group sings these words to the tune of "Skip to My Lou":

Here comes (red) now what'll we do?
Here comes (red) now what'll we do?
Here comes (red) now what'll we do?
Skip around. That's what we'll do.

The child in the center then pulls out another color and the game continues.

Objective To recognize the letter *u*, to say its short-vowel sound, as in *up*, and to write the letter correctly.

Understandings The letter *u* represents eight different vowel sounds in English. It represents the *uh* sound in *up* six times more often than the next most frequent sound, as in *pull*, and nine times more often than the *you* sound in *use*. Teaching the short-vowel sound first gives children a more useful tool for early independent writing.

Materials

itl puppet

Audiocassette, Side 1, "*uggy duck*"

Character Cards 1, 13, 14

my itl book Activity 13, one per child

crayons

newsprint—one large, easel-sized sheet

black, felt-tipped pen

Story

Display the character cards as you either tell the story or play the recording.

uggy duck

It was early morning in *itl*'s garden. *ed* had spent the night with *itl*. He went to sleep, dreaming of all the letters and sounds he had learned.

In the morning, *ed* awoke first. "What are all those noises?" he called. "It sounds like I'm back at the zoo!"

"It's just the animals from the farm down the road," *itl* told him. "They always make a lot of noise when they wake up."

ed thought about the noises. Each of *itl*'s friends made a special sound. And *itl* had shown him how to make the letters that stand for those sounds. "*itl*," said *ed*, "do you suppose there are letters for the sounds those farm animals make?"

"Sure," said *itl*. "On the way back to the zoo, we'll take a shortcut through the farm. Then I can introduce you to some of my friends and help you write their letters."

Right after breakfast *itl* and *ed* started off to the zoo by way of the farm. Just inside the gate they heard this sound: "uh-uh-uh-uh."

ed stopped in his tracks. "Is that little duck making that strange sound?" he asked.

itl nodded. "That's *uggy*. One of the bigger ducks accidentally stepped on him when he was hatching, and he lost his breath. The other ducks have tried to teach him to quack, but he still sounds like he's out of breath."

"Do you know how to make *uggy*'s letter, *itl*?" *ed* asked.

"*uggy*'s letter looks almost like he does," laughed *itl* as he wrote it in the sand next to the duck.

ed slowly wrote the letter with the stick held in his trunk, and *uggy* added the sound: "uh-uh-uh!"

ed smiled. "Yes," he thought, "an extra-long trunk is really useful for writing. I wonder what other letters I can learn at the farm?"

Activity

Write the letter *u* in the air, describing each stroke: "Straight down, around, and up again. Then straight down." Repeat several times with the children, making the /u/ sound together as you write the letter.

Distribute the tear-out section of *my itl book* Activity 13 and black crayons. Have children write their initials on the *GO* side at the top of their paper. Demonstrate the steps in drawing *uggy* on a large sheet of newsprint as the children complete their drawing.

Draw *uggy*'s letter, adding his head, body, and feet as shown:

Then add the talking balloon and write *u* in it as you say the /u/ sound.

Tell children to make three more of *uggy*'s letters below his picture.

Check Point

Go from child to child and ask each one to make the new speech sound and to write the new letter. Watch for straight sides on the *u*. If necessary, remind children that this letter starts with a standing line, not a curve.

Record individual performance on the Progress Checklist.

Extended Activities

1. Distribute *my itl books* and crayons. Have children turn to page 13. Tell them to trace the letter and to write a *u* in the balloon as they make the sound. Then have them color *uggy*.

2. Give each child a copy of Activity Sheet 22, crayons, and scissors. Have children color and cut out *uggy*. Then help them attach the cutout to a folded strip of construction paper or a wooden stick, to make a stick puppet. The stick puppets may be used to enact the story.

3. Add the new sound and letter to the activities you've already established: Tello game, Look-and-Do strips, feely boxes, magnetic letters, Hop-Spell game.

4. Teach the hand sign for the letter *u*.

5. Encourage children to form *uggy*'s letter with their body, saying his sound as they make the letter.

6. Choose volunteers to pantomime the story as you retell it, or to dramatize it using their own words.

7. Touch-write the letter *u* on children's backs, asking them to say the sound you write.

8. Play the Chair Game using the five short-vowel sounds. (See Extended Activities in Lesson 26.) Begin by demonstrating that the /u/ sound is a "jaw dropper" sound, like /a/ and /o/. Ask them to rest their chin on the back of their hand and to feel their chin drop lower as they make the three sounds—/u/, /a/, and /o/. Tell children to read your lips and to do the following actions as you say the words without making any sound.

> *at* (stand beside their chair)
> *in* (sit in their chair)
> *on* (put a foot on their chair)
> *edge* (sit on the edge of their chair)
> *under* (put a foot under their chair)

9. Play "Stepping-Stones." Materials: 20 large file cards, black, felt-tipped pen. Print the five vowel letters on large file cards, printing each letter on about four separate cards. Place the cards in stepping-stone fashion in front of your playground exit. When children are excused, have them make the vowel sounds as they walk next to the cards. Note which children and which sounds need more practice.

10. Have children play Tello with vowel sounds, using the five short-vowel sounds already taught. Materials: Cards 1, 2, 11, 12, 21-26. Listen to see that children *say* the sounds and don't just visually match the cards.

LESSON 30

Objective To draw rainbow curves from left to right.

> ***Understandings*** This is an easy task for most young children. It is a separate lesson because this writing stroke is a major part of the construction of the next group of letters (*r, n, h, m, p*). If children's writing progress is going well, you might want to increase the pace to three letters a week.

Materials

   itl puppet
   Activity Sheet 23, one copy per child
   Character Cards 1, 13
   blue, red, and yellow crayons, water colors, or tempera paint
   crayons (eight standard colors) for each child
   newsprint—one large, easel-sized sheet

Story

   Display the character cards as you tell the story. Draw a rainbow on the newsprint with crayons, water colors, or tempera paint as *ed* draws the rainbow in the story.

itl and ed make a rainbow

   Soon after *itl* and *ed* met *uggy* at the farm, it started to rain. *itl* and *ed* ran back to *itl*'s house to wait until the storm was over. It rained so hard that *itl*'s roof kept leaking. They put pans on the floor underneath all the leaks! When the pans filled up, *itl* and *ed* carried them outside and emptied them. Then they put them back under the leaks. It was hard work!

   At last the rain stopped and the sun came out. The sun shone through the raindrops that were still falling in the distance and made a beautiful rainbow. *itl* and *ed* went outside to see it. They counted seven colors in the rainbow. It was red at the top, then orange, yellow, green, light blue, dark blue, and at the bottom, it was purple.

   It was so pretty that *ed* wanted to draw a rainbow just like it. *itl* went in-side to get some paper and crayons. When he came back, he told *ed*, "We can't color a rainbow. I can only find three crayons—a red, a yellow, and a blue. We need to have seven colors for a rainbow."

   "We can make a rainbow anyway," *ed* said. "I'll show you how to do it."

   ed took the red crayon in his trunk. (Move your arm from the children's left to their right as you draw each stripe.) With a big sweep, he made a fat round stripe, starting at the bottom on the *GO* side, going up high, and then going down to the bottom of the *STOP* side, like the top of a circle.

   Then *ed* took a yellow crayon and made a fat yellow stripe that blended into the red stripe. Where the red and yellow met, there was an orange stripe!

ed did the same thing with a blue crayon. Where the blue and yellow blended, there was a green stripe!

ed pushed harder with the blue crayon to make a dark blue stripe. At the bottom of his blue stripe, he added some red to make it purple.

"You are the smartest elephant in the whole world," *itl* told *ed*. "You made a seven-colored rainbow with only three crayons!"

Activity

Give each child a copy of Activity Sheet 23 and crayons. Tell children to look at the word on each curved line and then to use that color to make a line of the rainbow. If children aren't sure of the words, you might remind them to match the words with the words on the crayons, or you could write the words on each band of the newsprint rainbow drawn during the story.

When they have finished the rainbow, have children draw *itl* and *ed* below the rainbow. If necessary, demonstrate the drawings using the illustrations in Lessons 6 and 26.

Check Point

While children are finishing their rainbows, go from child to child and ask each one to make the rainbow curve in the air for you, going from left to right.

Record individual performance on the Progress Checklist.

Extended Activities

1. Have children use fingerpaint to make rainbows on construction paper. Give them only three colors—blue, red, and yellow—to blend into a seven-color rainbow, as *ed* did in the story.

2. Use a prism in the sunlight to make a rainbow on a light-colored wall. Point out the color sequence.

Objective To recognize the letter *r*, to say its speech sound, and to write the letter correctly.

Understandings Some speech pathologists distinguish between the sound represented by *r* at the beginning of words and its sound at the end of words. There is a slight difference in emphasis: the beginning /r/ is usually stronger than the ending /r/ in standard American English. In some regional dialects this is more obvious. For purposes of this program, the speech sounds at the beginning of *red* and the ending of *car* are the same.

The /r/ sound is one of the most difficult to make in any language. When a task is difficult, young children sometimes avoid it by substituting an easier task. For example, rather than make a concerted effort to learn to skip on alternate feet, some children continue to gallop instead, so that they do not have to change feet. Another common substitution is when children who have midline difficulty turn the paper to avoid making horizontal lines. The most common substitution that children make for the /r/ sound is /oo/ (*oo-ed* for *red*). Children who have acquired this speech habit need help to overcome it but shouldn't be told that they are saying it wrong. Instead, when a child is substituting /oo/, look directly at the child and repeat the sentence with the correct sound. For example, if one of your students says "oo-ead me the oo-abbit stowee," repeat the child's words pronouncing the words correctly, "Yes, I'll read the rabbit story." Deliberately *smile* when you make the /r/ sounds. Gradually the child will imitate your facial expression. It is physically impossible to say /oo/ with a smile on your face.

The strokes used to write *r* are the foundation strokes for the rest of the "stick-rainbow" letters that follow:

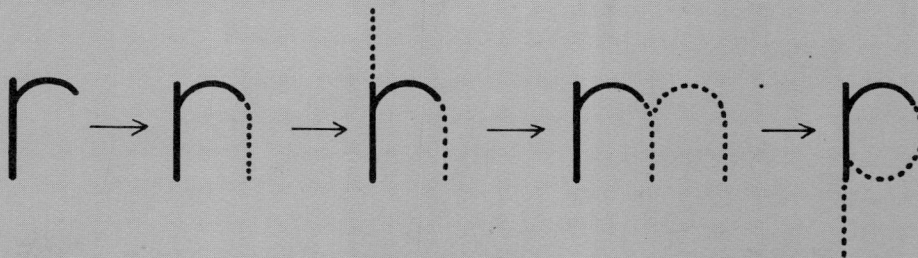

$$r \rightarrow n \rightarrow h \rightarrow m \rightarrow p$$

At this point, children have begun to trace letter strokes when they write the last stroke for *a*, *g*, and *u*. A few children may be able to trace the downward stick on *d* without leaving a gap. The next five letters, however, present a new, harder tracing task: *It is more difficult to trace a line going away from the body (uphill) than one that is going toward the body.* Part of the problem is that the writing hand covers the line being traced. The eye cannot control the execution of this task. Beginners who write too·fast will make letters like flying birds or rounded *v*'s. Others will not complete their rainbow stroke to curve it downhill. Continue to have these children practice until they can trace strokes correctly.

Materials

itl puppet
Audiocassette, Side 2, "*rusty rooster*"
Character Cards 1, 13, 15
my itl book Activity 14, one per child
black writing crayons, one per child
crayons
newsprint—one large, easel-sized sheet
black, felt-tipped pen

Story

Display the character cards as you either tell the story or play the recording.

rusty rooster

After *itl* had introduced *ed* to *uggy*, the two friends heard another sound: "r-r-r-r."

"Now that sounds like the farmer trying to start his tractor," *ed* said.
itl laughed. "That's *rusty* rooster, learning to crow. He knows how to make the sound, but for a proper crow, you have to do it five times in a row. And that's where *rusty* has trouble. He can't count to five."

ed looked at *rusty* clutching the rail fence with his feet and trying to crow.

Suddenly *ed* had an idea. "Maybe I can help *rusty*," he said.
itl introduced *ed* to the weary little rooster and *ed* showed *rusty* how to keep track of the sounds by counting to five on his toes. In no time at all *rusty* was crowing like a regular rooster: "r-r-r-r-r . . . !"

Then *itl* showed *ed* how to write *rusty*'s letter. First he made a standing line and then he traced the line almost to the top and made a rainbow line.

ed worked and worked to make the letter. Tracing the stick line was the hardest part, but finally he could do it without leaving a space between the lines. He added the rainbow line and stood back to look at what he'd done. Then he said, "It's hard to know which is more fun—learning something new, or teaching someone something new."

rusty rooster proudly crowed, "r-r-r-r-r."
itl smiled, "Well, it's easy to tell what *rusty* thinks is more fun!"

Activity

Ask children to make *rusty*'s sound, raising a finger for each /r/. Repeat several times. Then write the letter *r* in the air, describing the strokes: "Make a standing line, trace the standing line almost to the top, and make a little rainbow line." Repeat, having children write the letter in the air as you describe the strokes.

Distribute the tear-out section of *my itl book* Activity 14. Have children write their initials on the *GO* side at the top of their paper. Demonstrate how to draw *rusty* on a large sheet of newsprint as children complete their drawing.

Draw *rusty*'s letter, head, body, tail, and feet as shown.

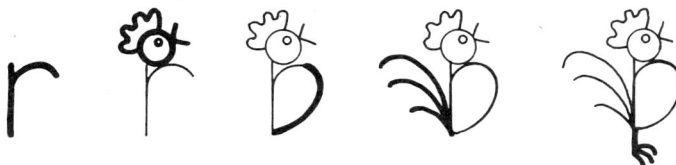

Add the talking balloon and write *rusty*'s letter in it as you say the sound.

Tell children to write several more of *rusty*'s letter on the lines below the picture, making *rusty*'s sound as they write each one. Then have them color *rusty*.

Check Point

As children are drawing, go from child to child, asking each one to make the new sound and to write the letter *r*.

Record individual performance on the Progress Checklist.

Extended Activities

1. Distribute *my itl books* and crayons. Have children turn to page 14. Tell them to trace *rusty*'s letter and then to write the letter in the balloon. Have them color *rusty*.

2. Give each child a copy of Activity Sheet 24, crayons, and scissors. Have children color and cut out *rusty*. Then help them attach the cutout to a folded strip of construction paper or a wooden stick, to make a stick puppet. The stick puppets may be used to enact the story.

3. Add the new sound and letter to activities you've already established: Tello game, Look-and-Do strips, objects that begin with the /r/ sound, feely boxes, magnetic letters, Hop-Spell game.

4. Teach the hand sign for the letter *r*.

5. Have children form *rusty*'s letter with their body, saying *rusty*'s sound as they make the letter.

6. Choose volunteers to replay the story, pantomiming it as you retell it or dramatizing it in their own words.

7. Give children newsprint and black crayons. Use these words in a dictation exercise: *red, rats, rugs, rod*.

8. Show children who have learned all the letters in their name how to write their name correctly.

9. Send home Parent Letter 8 with the child's name written in the *itl* script.

10. If children are associating the word *left* with the *GO* side, start using the word *right*. An association that's useful in teaching children this word is that most children write with their right hands.

Play Simon Says using the words *left* and *right* instead of *GO* and *STOP*. If children are confused by the new words, go back to using *GO* and *STOP* and teach *left* and *right* later.

Lesson 32

Objective To recognize the letter *n*, to say its speech sound, and to write the letter correctly.

Understandings The /n/ is an easy speech sound to make. It occurs in most languages of the world, and infants make it quite early in development. It is the first sound of the *itl Early Writing Program* that reverberates through the nose.

The letter *n* is made exactly like the letter *r*, except the rainbow goes all the way down to the ground line. Writing these two letters on wide-lined paper for practice will help children write them more distinctively. Some children may try to avoid the tracing of the stick by simply making a hump and then adding a "chimney" on the top left. This habit, of course, will prevent later fluency. Letters formed with incorrect stroke sequences shouldn't be accepted, no matter how neat the final result looks.

Materials

> *itl* puppet
> Audiocassette, Side 2, "*nosey nag*"
> Character Cards 1, 13, 16
> *my itl book* Activity 15, one per child
> black writing crayons, one per child
> crayons
> newsprint—one large, easel-sized sheet
> black, felt-tipped pen

Story

Display the character cards as you either tell the story or play the recording.

nosey nag

itl and *ed* kept strolling through the farm, listening for the sounds of *itl*'s friends.

All at once *ed* stopped. "Listen!" he said. "Somebody's laughing at us."

itl listened, too: "n-n-n-n-n," they heard.

"That's *nosey* nag," said *itl*, hurrying in the direction of the sound. "She's the farmer's horse. But she's retired now. She gives rides to children who come to the farm. She really enjoys the children. That's why she laughs a lot."

As they came around the corner of the barn, they saw a young child stroking *nosey*'s face while *nosey* laughed quietly: "n-n-n-n-n."

When *itl* introduced *ed*, *nosey* said, "Hello, *ed*. This is my new friend Tyler. He'd like a ride, but there's no one here to put him on my back."

"Why, that's something I can do," *ed* said. With his trunk he easily swung Tyler onto *nosey*'s back. *nosey* carried Tyler 'round and 'round the barnyard, snickering happily: "n-n-n-n-n!"

Meanwhile, *itl* showed *ed* how to make *nosey*'s letter. "Like *rusty rooster's*," he said, "but you make the rainbow line come all the way down to the ground."

ed tried it a few times until the letter he made looked just right. By then *nosey* had had enough exercise for one day. She trotted back so that *ed* could lift Tyler down again. *itl* and *ed* waved good-bye to *nosey* and set off to follow other sounds. Behind them they could still hear *nosey* laughing with Tyler: "n-n-n-n!"

Activity

Ask children to make *nosey*'s sound. Show them that the tongue position is very similar to that for /t/, /d/, and /l/. Emphasize the "nosy" sound that we hear at the beginning of *nose* by telling children to hold their nose shut with their fingers and try to say /nnnnnnnnnn/. The /n/ sound won't come out because the nose is closed. This will help them distinguish the /n/ sound from the other nasal speech sounds taught later.

Write the letter *n* in the air, describing the strokes: "Make a standing line . . . trace the standing line almost to the top, and then make a rainbow line." Repeat, having children write the letter in the air and describe the strokes with you.

Distribute the tear-out section of *my itl book* Activity 15 and black crayons. Have children write their initials on the *GO* side at the top of their paper. Demonstrate the steps in drawing *nosey* on a large sheet of newsprint as children complete their drawing.

Draw *nosey*'s letter, adding her head, body, tail, and mane as shown:

Then add the talking balloon and write *n* in it as you say the /n/ sound.

Tell children to write several more of *nosey*'s letter below their drawing. Then have them color *nosey*.

Check Point

While children are drawing, go from child to child and ask each one to make the new sound and to write the letter. Make notes of children who still need more practice.

Record individual performance on the Progress Checklist.

Extended Activities

1. Distribute *my itl books* and crayons. Have children turn to page 15. Tell them to trace the letter and to write an *n* in the balloon. Then have them color *nosey* as they say her sound.

2. Give each child a copy of Activity Sheet 25, crayons, and scissors. Have children color and cut out *nosey.* Then help them attach the cutout to a folded strip of construction paper or a wooden stick, to make a stick puppet. The puppets may be used to enact the story.

3. Add the new sound and letter to activities you've already established: Tello game, Look-and-Do strips, objects that begin with the /n/ sound, feely boxes, magnetic letters, Hop-Spell game.

4. Teach the hand sign for the letter *n.*

5. Have children form *nosey*'s letter with their body, saying her sound as they make the letter.

6. Choose volunteers to play *itl, ed,* and *nosey* nag; have them pantomime the story as you retell it or dramatize it using their own words.

7. Give children newsprint and black crayons. Use these words in a dictation exercise: *ten, tin, sun, net, not, nut.*

8. Draw faces. Give each child newsprint and crayons. Begin by asking a few children to sit in front of the group. Ask children to describe the shape of a head. If children respond with "round," ask them if the chin area is as wide as the forehead and top of the head. Point out that heads are oval-shaped, more like an egg than a ball. Demonstrate the steps in drawing a face; have children copy each step.

Draw an oval on the paper.

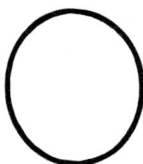

Ask children where the ears are on a head; draw the ears near the middle of the oval.

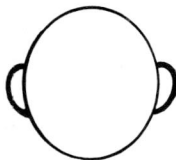

Repeat for the eyes. (Many young children put the eyes in the forehead area; show them that eyes are at about the same level as the top of the ears.)

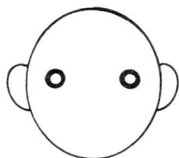

Ask children where the nose is; draw an *n* in the middle of the face for the nose.

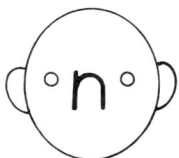

Tell children you are going to draw an open mouth that is making the /n/ sound. Draw two smile lines, one under the other. Draw a large talking balloon and write the word *no* in the balloon.

Show children how to make an exclamation point after the word *no*. Point out that the exclamation point is made with a straight line and a dot and it looks like an upside-down *itl*. Explain that the exclamation point means that the word or sentence should be said in a loud or excited voice. Give some examples of exclamatory statements—"Fire!" "Happy Birthday!"

When children have finished, have them share their pictures and tell why the person is saying *no*.

9. Play music for galloping while children gallop around the room like *nosey*. When the music stops, they are to stop galloping and make *nosey*'s sound.

LESSON 33

Objective To recognize the letter *h*, to say its sound, and to write the letter correctly.

Understandings This letter isn't voiced; it is not *huh*. The /h/ sound is a "whisper" sound, a breath of exhaled air, the same sound a tired, panting dog makes. Most young children have observed dogs doing this and can easily imitate the sound. Other "whisper" sounds already taught are /c/, /f/, /s/, /t/.

The letter *h* is an excellent example of the weak relationship between alphabet letter names and their common speech sounds in written English. Knowing that this symbol is called *aych* doesn't help a child learn to write and read. In fact, such knowledge often gets in the way of using this letter correctly.

Materials

itl puppet
Audiocassette, Side 2, "*hamilton hound*"
Character Cards 1, 13, 17
my itl book Activity 16, one per child
black writing crayons, one per child
crayons
newsprint—one large, easel-sized sheet
black, felt-tipped pen

Story

Display the character cards as you either tell the story or play the recording.

hamilton hound

After they left *nosey* nag, *ed* was surprised to see a huge, floppy-eared hound dog running straight toward them, wagging his head from side to side.

"Oh-oh!" said *ed.* "We'd better watch out. This fellow looks dangerous!"

"Don't worry!" said *itl.* "That's *hamilton*, the farmer's hound dog. He's really just a big, playful puppy."

hamilton skidded to a stop, nearly toppling *itl* over, and tried to catch his breath: "h-h-h-h-h-h."

While *hamilton* was lying on the grass, trying to get his breath, *itl* was busy showing *ed* how to write *hamilton*'s letter. "Why look at that!" *ed* exclaimed. "It's just like *nosey*'s letter—only taller."

By now *ed* had learned a lot of new letters from the farm animals and he was beginning to think it was time to get back to the zoo. He was eager to show the other elephants what he had learned. But *itl* had a few more friends for *ed* to meet, so they said good-bye to *hamilton* and started on.

"How many letters can a fellow carry in his head?" *ed* wondered, as he tapped his head lightly with his trunk.

"Oh, well," he smiled, "I guess there's still room for more."

Activity

Write the letter *h* in the air, describing the strokes: "Start with a tall stick. Trace your line up the stick about halfway. Next, draw a rainbow all the way down." Repeat, having children write the letter in the air with you as they make *hamilton*'s sound.

Distribute the tear-out section of *my itl book* Activity 16 and black crayons. Have children write their initials on the *GO* side at the top of their paper. Demonstrate the steps in drawing *hamilton* on a large sheet of newsprint as the children complete their drawing.

Draw the letter *h*, adding *hamilton*'s head, body, and tail as shown:

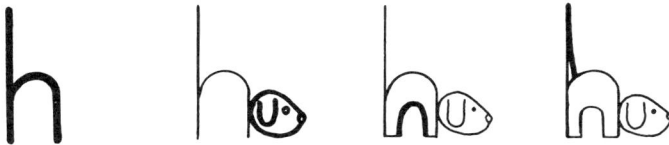

Add the talking balloon and write *h* in it as you say the sound.

Tell children to write *hamilton*'s letter several times below the picture. Then have them color *hamilton*.

Check Point

Ask each child to make the new speech sound and to write the letter. Make note of any children who still need practice, especially those who do not start with a tall stick, or who do not retrace uphill. Remind children to retrace halfway up the stick. Retracing should be done slowly. Turning their wrist slightly will help children see what they are doing.

Record individual performance on the Progress Checklist.

Extended Activities

1. Distribute *my itl books* and crayons. Have children turn to page 16. Tell them to trace the letter and then to write the letter in the balloon as they say *hamilton*'s sound. Then have them color *hamilton*.

2. Give each child a copy of Activity Sheet 26, crayons, and scissors. Have children color and cut out *hamilton*. Then help them attach the cutout to a folded strip of construction paper or a wooden stick. The puppets may be used to enact the story.

3. Add the new sound and letter to activities you've already established: Tello game, Look-and-Do strips, objects that begin with the /h/ sound, feely boxes, magnetic letters, Hop-Spell game.

4. Teach the hand sign for the letter *h*.

5. Have children form *hamilton*'s letter with their body, saying his sound as they make the letter.

6. Choose volunteers to play *itl*, *ed*, and *hamilton*. Have them pantomime the story as you retell it or dramatize it using their own words.

7. Give children newsprint and black crayons. Dictate some of the following sentences for children to write on newsprint. Remind children to use spaces between words; after you dictate a word, say "space" and pause. Remind children to use a period at the end of each sentence. Some children will need help decoding their sentences after they have written them. Show them how to run their fingers under the words, saying each word slowly, sound by sound. Repeat, doing it faster each time. Reading is harder than writing from dictation. If a child says, "I don't remember," encourage the child to *look* at each letter and *say* its sound.

fred hops to *ed.*	it is hot.
jac jogs to *itl.*	*itl* is in his sand.
gus ran to *dot.*	*dot* runs to *lit.*
dad cut his hand.	*dot* has dots.

Encourage children to illustrate the sentences.

8. A number of the children will be able to write their name with the letters that have been introduced. Work with children individually to help them learn to write their name.

LESSON 34

Objective To recognize the letter *m*, to say its speech sound, and to write the letter correctly.

Understandings This is a nasal sound, like *n*, but it is made with the mouth closed, whereas /n/ is made with the mouth open. Point out this difference to children, reminding them to watch your face during dictation exercises. If they depend only on their ears, they are more likely to make mistakes.

This sound is made very early in infancy, so children will have no trouble making it in any language. Have children who still need help watch their mouths in a mirror as they hum. The /m/ sound isn't preceded or followed by a vowel; it is not *em* or *muh*.

If children can write the letter *n*, then *m* will be easy for them to learn. To make the *m* correctly, however, they must retrace the first two vertical strokes so the humps aren't sprawled out.

Materials

itl puppet
Audiocassette, Side 2, "*molly mosquito*"
Character Cards 1, 13, 18
my itl book Activity 17, one per child
black writing crayons, one per child
crayons
newsprint—one large, easel-sized sheet
black, felt-tipped pen

Story

Display the character cards as you either tell the story or play the recording.

molly mosquito

itl and *ed* were still at the farm when suddenly *ed* raised his long trunk high in the air. "Aha! There's a sound I recognize. m-m-m-m-m-m. It's a mosquito! Just wait till it gets closer and I'll swat it with my trunk," he said.

"Oh, no!" cried *itl*. "That's no ordinary mosquito. It's *molly*, and she's a friend."

itl explained that *molly* had a problem with her stinger. *molly* was born with such a short stinger that she couldn't sting! Since she couldn't hurt anyone, all the farm animals had learned to love her and liked to listen to her merry humming.

Just then *molly* flew in and settled down to meet *ed*. While *itl* showed *ed* how to write *molly*'s letter, *molly* hummed her favorite song. "m-m-m-m."

itl showed *ed* how to write *molly*'s letter by adding a rainbow to *nosey*'s letter. *molly*'s music made *ed* think of m-m-mountains and m-m-meadows, and m-m-moonbeams, and m-m-magic. Before long, *molly*'s humming put *ed* and *itl* to sleep. *molly* left them to finish their nap and hummed away: "m-m-m-m-m."

Activity

Tell children to say *molly*'s sound and to feel the two bumps on their top lip while they make the sound. Then write the letter *m* in the air, describing the strokes. Repeat, asking children to write the letter in the air with you as they say the sound.

Distribute the tear-out section of *my itl book* Activity 17 and black crayons. Demonstrate the steps in drawing *molly* on a large sheet of newsprint as the children complete their drawing.

Trace *molly*'s letter, adding her head, legs, and wings as shown.

Add the talking balloon and write *m* in it as you say the sound.

Have children write several *m*'s below the picture and then color *molly*.

Check Point

Ask each child to make the new sound and to write the letter. If children are having difficulty retracing the lines, show them how to turn their wrist slightly so they can see the lines to be retraced.

Record individual performance on the Progress Checklist.

Extended Activities

1. Distribute *my itl books* and crayons. Have children turn to page 17. Tell them to trace the letter and then to write it in the balloon. Encourage them to say *molly*'s sound as they write the letter and then to color *molly*.

2. Give each child a copy of Activity Sheet 27, crayons, and scissors. Have children color and cut out *molly*. Then help them attach the cutout to a folded strip of construction paper or a wooden stick, to make a stick puppet. The stick puppets may be used to enact the story.

3. Add the new sound and letter to activities you've already established: Tello game, Look-and-Do strips, objects that begin with the /m/ sound, feely boxes, magnetic letters, Hop-Spell game.

4. Teach the hand sign for the letter *m*.

5. Encourage children to form *molly*'s letter with their body, saying her sound as they make the letter.

6. Choose volunteers to play *itl*, *ed*, and *molly*. Have them pantomime the story as you retell it or dramatize it using their own words.

7. Distribute newsprint and black crayons. Dictate sentences that include the new letter and sound. Have children listen to each sentence, repeat it, and then write it.

> it is mom.
> mom is mad.
> dad met mom.
> Have children illustrate the sentences.

8. Distribute newsprint and black crayons. Use these words for dictation. Following the dictation, help children read the words back aloud. Remind them to run their fingers slowly under each word, from left to right, as they make each sound and to listen to each sound.

man	mug	hem	him
men	ham	dim	mud
gum	rim	met	hum
mom	mad	mat	jam

9. Play "Skin the Cat." Materials: yardstick or broomstick for each child. Lead the activity, demonstrating each part: Hold the stick in front of you with both hands. Step over the stick with one foot, then the other. The stick is now behind you. Bring the stick up behind you, until it is over your head. Now, return the stick to the starting place. The more control children have of their body, the easier letter writing will be. This activity is a good indoor exercise when weather won't permit outdoor activities.

LESSON 35

Objective To recognize the letter *p*, to make its speech sound, as in *up*, and to write the letter correctly.

Understandings The /p/ sound is another unvoiced "whisper" sound; it is neither *pea* nor *puh*. This letter isn't difficult to teach if you take it step by step: The rainbow curve begins at approximately the same place as the curve for *r, n, h,* and *m* (not quite up to the top of the stick). For this letter, however, the rainbow keeps curving into a circle until it hits the stick line.

Materials

> *itl* puppet
> Audiocassette, Side 2, "*piggy*"
> Character Cards 1, 13, 19
> *my itl book* Activity 18, one per child
> black writing crayons, one per child
> crayons
> newsprint—one large, easel-sized sheet
> black, felt-tipped pen

Story

Display the character cards as you either tell the story or play the recording.

piggy

itl and *ed* were still sleeping from *molly* mosquito's magic music when they were suddenly wakened by a new sound: "p-p-p-p-p." ·

ed jumped to his feet. "Is that a motorboat?" he cried.

"No," said *itl*. "That's *piggy*. She's so plump that she can't see her feet and she sometimes steps in holes. When she does, she bangs her chin on the ground and gets dust all over her face." *itl* went on to explain that while some pigs liked dirt, *piggy* didn't! She spent most of her time blowing the dust from her face and her feet.

Sure enough, across the barnyard came a very round little pig, stumbling from hole to hole, all the while blowing dust off her face: "p-p-p-p-p."

When *itl* introduced *ed* to *piggy*, she cried, "P-p-p-poor me! Some of this dust seems to be p-p-pasted to my skin. I can't p-p-poof it off! I do hate to be dirty."

ed had an idea. Next to the barn was a large tank of water for *nosey*. *ed* went to the tank and filled his trunk with water. Then, holding his trunk high over his head, he carried the water back to *piggy* and gave her a shower. The water washed away all of the dried-on dirt and left her pink and shiny and smiling. She sat in the sun to dry while *itl* showed *ed* how to write her letter: a low-hanging stick line, traced almost to the top, and then a rainbow line around and back to the stick.

By the time *ed* had learned to make the letter, *piggy* was dry and was again softly blowing the dust from her face: "p-p-p-p-p." It was easy to see that she thought *ed* was a very special elephant.

Activity

Show children how to make *piggy*'s sound: Close your lips, then force out air in a slight puff, as if blowing dust away from your face as *piggy* does in the story.

Then write the letter *p* in the air, describing the strokes: "Make a stick line and come back up the line, almost to the top. Start your rainbow. Curl your rainbow around until it hits the stick." Repeat, having children write the letter in the air with you, making *piggy*'s sound as they make the letter.

Distribute the tear-out section of *my itl book* Activity 18 and black crayons. Have children write their initials on the *GO* side at the top of their paper. Demonstrate the steps in drawing *piggy* on a large sheet of newsprint as the children complete their drawing.

Trace *piggy*'s letter, adding her head, body, feet, and tail as shown:

Add the talking balloon and write *p* in it as you say the sound.

Tell the children to write three more of *piggy*'s letter, reminding them that her stick falls below "ground" (bottom line), just like *piggy* when she falls in holes. Then have them color *piggy*.

Check Point

While children are completing their drawing, go from child to child and ask each one to make the new sound and to write the letter. This is a difficult letter to make; watch for children who need extra practice.

Record individual performance on the Progress Checklist.

Extended Activities

1. Distribute *my itl books* and crayons. Have children turn to page 18. Tell them to trace the letter and then to write a *p* in the balloon as they say *piggy*'s sound. Have them color *piggy*.

2. Give each child a copy of Activity Sheet 28, crayons, and scissors. Have children color and cut out *piggy*. Then help them attach the cutout to a folded strip of construction paper or a wooden stick, to make a stick puppet. The stick puppets may be used to enact the story.

3. Add the new sound and letter to activities you've already established: Tello game, Look-and-Do strips, objects that begin with the /p/ sound, feely boxes, magnetic letters, and Hop-Spell game.

4. Teach the hand sign for the letter *p*.

5. Have children form *piggy*'s letter with their body, saying her sound as they make the letter.

6. Choose volunteers to play *itl*, *ed*, and *piggy*. Have them pantomime the story as you retell it, or dramatize it using their own words.

7. Give children newsprint and black crayons. Use some of these words in dictation exercises. Remind children that *piggy*'s stick falls below the other letters.

hop	pot	pat	pig	*fred* can hop.
tip	pad	past	pig pen	*jac* can jump.
tap	pal	pet	piglet	*hamilton* can pant.
help!	pan	pit	peg	
pep	pant	pen	pin	
pod	pants			

8. Let the children help you make popcorn. Materials: popcorn popper, popcorn, and oil. Every time they hear a kernel pop, encourage them to make the /p/ sound. Explain to them that when the moisture in the corn kernels gets hot, it makes steam inside. The steam has no way to get out, so finally the kernels explode. When the children make the /p/ sound, their lips are closed. There is no way for air to get out, so it just explodes, making the /p/ sound.

Objective To recognize the letter *b*, to say its sound, as in *tub*, and to write the letter correctly.

Understandings This speech sound is made exactly like the /p/ sound except it vibrates the "voice box." Children can contrast these two sounds by placing their fingers on the front of their throat and feeling the vibration on the /b/.

Children must be able to make the letter *d* correctly before the *b* is introduced. If they haven't internalized the *d* before learning the *b*, they may confuse these two letters and be slowed considerably in future writing, reading, and spelling activities. If your children are making the letter *d* circle-first, toward the *GO* (left) side, have internalized the *d* shape through regular practice, and are correctly associating the /d/ sound with the letter, then teach the letter *b*. If, on the other hand, your students persist in making a stick-first *d*, stop and teach them the correct form for *d* before teaching this lesson.

Communication with parents about the correct form for *d* is important; if parents are accepting a stick-first *d* in home practice, the child will see no need to change. If children are shown how to make these two letters correctly, they will be able to distinguish them kinetically, without depending on vision.

The formation of the *b* in this lesson is the foundation for the joined cursive *b* that children will be expected to use in the intermediate years of school. By learning it this way, they will have no need to change at a later date. The addition of the little "feather" at this point prepares children for joining this letter to others. More important, the feather stroke helps to distinguish this letter from *d*. Children who still have not acquired laterality cannot distinguish visually the difference between objects oriented to the right and objects oriented to the left. The more ways these two mirror-image letters are different, the easier it will be for beginners to distinguish them.

b d

Materials

itl puppet
Audiocassette, Side 2, "*bud bird*"
Character Cards 1, 13, 20
my itl book Activity 19, one per child
black writing crayons, one per child
crayons
newsprint—one large, easel-sized sheet
black, felt-tipped pen

Story

Display the character cards as you either tell the story or play the recording.

bud bird

As *itl* and *ed* walked away from *piggy*, her sound was suddenly replaced by another sound. "Listen," said *ed*, stretching his big elephant ears. "It sounds like somebody is very cold." *itl* listened. He, too, heard someone making a shivery sound, like this: "b-b-b-b-b-b-b."

The sound was coming from a baby bird, shivering and crying. He hadn't grown enough feathers to keep warm.

"Why, that's *bud*," said *itl*. "I wonder what he's doing outside the nest." The three friends hurried over to the little bird and *itl* asked him where he was going.

bud pointed at a red *STOP* sign at the side of the road by the pasture. "Over there," he cried. "To my father." *bud*'s father was nowhere in sight, but suddenly *itl* knew what the problem was. *bud* was very young and couldn't see well yet. He saw the red *STOP* sign and thought it was his father's red stomach.

itl and *ed* couldn't convince *bud* that the sign was not his father, so they walked along with him toward the sign. As they walked, *ed* breathed through his trunk to warm the little bird. But because he was frightened, *bud* still shivered a little: "b-b-b-b-b." It seemed that *bud* had fallen out of the nest. He didn't have enough feathers to fly or even to keep warm, so he set out on foot to find his father—who was out looking for food.

itl wondered what would happen when they got to the stop sign and *bud* found that it wasn't his father. But just before they reached the sign, *bud*'s father flew up and landed beside it.

When *bud* saw his father, he turned to the others and said, "See? I knew it was Dad." Then he turned to his father and said, "They tried to tell me you were a *STOP* sign!"

bud's father took the little bird under his wing.

"b-b-b-b," shivered *bud*.

While *bud* warmed himself under his father's wing, *itl* showed *ed* how to make the letter for *bud*'s sound.

bud's father chirped his thanks.

And *bud* shivered happily: "b-b-b-b-b."

Activity

Make the letter *b* in the air, describing each stroke: "First make a tall stick. Stop at the bottom of the stick. Curl your line uphill toward the *STOP* sign, and then back toward the stick. Now make a little line sticking out." Repeat several times, asking children to make the letter in the air as they make *bud*'s sound.

Distribute the tear-out section of *my itl book* Activity 19 and black crayons. Have children write their initials on the *GO* side at the top of their paper. Demonstrate the steps in drawing *bud* on a large sheet of newsprint as the children complete their drawing.

Draw *bud*'s letter and add his head, tail, and legs as shown:

Add the talking balloon and write *b* in it as you make the sound.

Tell children to write three more of *bud*'s letter below the picture, making the sound as they write each letter. Have them color *bud*.

Check Point

While children are drawing, go from child to child and ask each one to make the new sound and to write the letter. If necessary, remind them to stop at the bottom of the straight line; this will help prevent them from rounding the corner so their letter looks like a 6.

Record individual performance on the Progress Checklist.

Extended Activities

1. Distribute *my itl books* and crayons. Have children turn to page 19. Tell them to trace the letter and to write a *b* in the balloon. Then have children make *bud*'s sound and color *bud*.

2. Give each child a copy of Activity Sheet 29, crayons, and scissors. Have children color and cut out *bud*. Then help them attach the cutout to a folded strip of construction paper or a wooden stick, to make a stick puppet. The stick puppets may be used to enact the story.

3. Add the new sound and letter to activities you've already established: Tello game, Look-and-Do strips, objects that begin with the /b/ sound, feely boxes, magnetic letters, Hop-Spell game.

4. Teach the hand sign for the letter *b*.

5. Have children form *bud*'s letter with their body, saying his sound as they make the letter.

6. Choose volunteers to play *itl*, *ed*, *bud*, and *bud*'s father. Have them pantomime the story as you retell it or dramatize it using their own words.

7. Distribute newsprint and black crayons. Dictate a few of these words and sentences daily until the *b-d* distinction is firmly established. Use some nonsense words. Ask children to read the words back.

big	bid	dog	rod
dig	deb	tab	rob
pig	lib	cub	bet
bad	tub	cud	*dot* is big.
bud	tud	bat	*lit* is red.
dub	ted	dat	it is *bud*.
rub	lid	bug	pig is fat.
red	teb	dug	
bed	bog	dad	

8. Sing an *itl* farm animal song to the tune of "Old MacDonald Had a Farm." Each verse changes to another farm animal (*rusty* rooster /r/, *hamilton* hound dog /h/, *molly* mosquito /m/, *piggy* /p/, *bud* bird /b/).

> *ed* and *itl* went to the farm
> /a//e//i//o//u/ (use short-vowel sounds)
> And on the farm they saw a duck
> /u//u//u//u//u/
> With an /u//u/ here and an /u//u/ there
> Here an /u/, there an /u/,
> Everywhere an /u/ /u/,
> *ed* and *itl* went to the farm
> /u//u//u//u//u/

LESSON 37

Objective To recognize the digraph *qu*, to say its sound, and to write *qu* correctly from dictation.

Understandings The letter *q* is always followed by the letter *u* in English, Spanish, and most of the other languages of the world. In Spanish and French, the *u* following *q* is silent. (In Spanish, *que* is pronounced *kay*, and in French, *quiche* is pronounced *keesh.*) In English, the *u* with *q* is pronounced /oo/.

We call two-letter combinations making a single sound *digraphs.* The Greeks invented digraphs because they didn't have enough alphabet letters for all the sounds in their language. They had no *f*, so they invented *ph*. In English, the word *digraph* is used to indicate other two-letter combinations that represent a single sound: *sh, th, ch, ll.* The combination *qu* is not a true digraph, because we hear two sounds rather than one. We pronounce both the consonant and the vowel, pronouncing *q* as /k/ and *u* as /oo/: coo-ick, for *quick*, coo-een, for *queen*, and coo-it for *quit.* Some individuals mistakenly add a third sound (coo-uh). Children need to know that the letter *q* is always followed by *u* in English, and that this two-letter combination is pronounced *coo.*

Materials

> *itl* puppet
> Audiocassette, Side 2, "*coo-coo quail*"
> Character Cards 1, 13, 14, 21
> *my itl book* Activity 20, one per child
> black writing crayons, one per child
> crayons
> newsprint—one large, easel-sized sheet
> black, felt-tipped pen

Story

Display the character cards as you either tell the story or play the recording.

coo-coo quail
The sun was high in the sky by the time *itl* and *ed* left the farm to head for the zoo. *ed* took one last look around to be sure he had seen everything he wanted to see.

"Wait a minute," *ed* said to *itl*. "I don't see *uggy* anywhere."

Just then, he spotted the duck far across the barnyard, walking along with a large brown bird at his heels. Together, the bird and *uggy* were making the strangest sound: "coo- coo- coo-coo."

"Who is that with *uggy*?" *ed* asked.

"Why that's *coo-coo* quail," said *itl*. "He lives in the meadow. He comes over here often to try to teach *uggy* to quack. *coo-coo* follows *uggy* all over the barnyard. You never see him without *uggy*. He keeps telling *uggy* the first part of quack. He says 'coo-coo-coo-coo.' *uggy* hasn't learned to do it yet."

145

"What's the matter with his leg?" *ed* asked *itl*.

"Well, when he was very young, the barn door closed on his foot. That's why it points in the wrong direction."

"Say *itl*, how do you write the letter for that sound?" *ed* asked.

"It's almost like *gus*'s letter, but the bottom of the stick bends the other way. Just like *coo-coo*'s foot," said *itl*.

Then with one last wave to everyone, *ed* and *itl* headed for the zoo.

Activity

Write the letter *q* in the air, describing the strokes. Then invite children to write the letter in the air along with you as they make *coo-coo*'s sound. Repeat several times.

Distribute the tear-out section of *my itl book* Activity 20 and black crayons. Have children write their initials on the *GO* side at the top of their paper. Demonstrate each step in drawing *coo-coo* on a large sheet of newsprint as children complete their drawing.

Draw *coo-coo*'s letter and add his head, feet, and tail as shown:

Then show children how to draw *uggy* next to *coo-coo* and write *qu* in the talking balloon.

Tell them to write *qu* beneath the picture several times, each time saying the sound as they write. Remind children that *coo-coo*'s leg goes below the line, like *gus*'s and *jac*'s. Then have them color *coo-coo*.

Check Point

While children are completing their drawings, go from child to child and ask each one to make the new sound and to write the two-letter combination.

Record individual performance on the Progress Checklist.

Extended Activities

1. Distribute *my itl books* and crayons. Have children turn to page 20. Tell them to trace the letter and to write *qu* in the balloon as they make *coo-coo*'s sound. Have them color *coo-coo*.

2. Give each child a copy of Activity Sheet 30, crayons, and scissors. Have children color and cut out *coo-coo*. Then help them attach the cutout to a folded strip of construction paper or a wooden stick, to make a stick puppet. The puppets may be used to enact the story.

3. Add the new sound and letter to the activities you've already established: Tello game, Look-and-Do strips, feely boxes, magnetic letters, and Hop-Spell game.

4. Teach the hand sign for the letter *q*.

5. Have children form *coo-coo*'s letter with their body, saying the sound as they make the letter.

6. Choose volunteers to play *itl*, *ed*, *uggy*, and *coo-coo*, either pantomiming the action or dramatizing it in their own words. To reinforce the idea that it takes two letters to make the new sound, tell *coo-coo* and *uggy* to bend over and grasp their ankles to walk like birds.

7. Give children newsprint and black crayons. Dictation practice for this sound is limited because the *qu* spelling pattern usually precedes the Latin (long-vowel) pronunciation of vowels. These words, however, can be used for dictation: *quit, quilt, squid, squint, quints, quest.*

8. Send home Parent Letter 9.

Objective To recognize the digraph *ng*, to say its sound, and to write *ng* correctly from dictation.

Understandings Now that *qu* has been introduced as a two-letter unit, other two-letter speech sounds will be easier to teach. This new combination, *ng*, is a true digraph. Its speech sound is common in English, usually as an ending. The three-letter unit, *ing*, shouldn't be taught until children are using *ng* correctly, or they may confuse the endings and misspell—for example, *saing* for *sang*. Teach *ng* instead with *a*, *i*, *o*, and *u*. English does not usually precede *ng* with *e* (except in the word *English*).

Materials

itl puppet

Character Cards 1, 8, 13, 16

black writing crayons or soft-lead pencils, one per child

crayons

gong or triangle rhythm instrument

newsprint, one 12″ x 15″ sheet per child

Story

Display the character cards as you tell the story.

nosey and gus

As they were leaving the farmyard, *itl* and *ed* were watching *nosey* nag eating grass near the farmer's milk shed.

Suddenly *nosey* looked up and saw *gus* grasshopper in front of her.

nosey was so frightened that she jumped backward, up in the air, and landed right on top of the milk shed!

The roof of the shed was metal. When her horseshoes landed there, they made this sound: "-ng-ng-ngngngngng." The noise startled *nosey* just as much as *gus* had, and she jumped off the milk shed as fast as she could.

gus hopped slowly over to *nosey*, trying not to scare her again. Then he opened his backpack and offered her some grape juice and a granola bar to help her calm down.

ed said, "That noise was so loud it's still ringing in my ears, ng-ng-ng-ng."

"It sounds like *nosey*'s sound and *gus*'s sound together," *itl* answered.

"Then I can write that sound!" *ed* said. Quickly, he picked up a stick in his trunk and wrote the letters in the dirt on the path. He looked at the letters and said the sound. "That's the sound *nosey* made when her horseshoes hit the milk shed roof, all right!"

Activity

Isolating this speech sound is easier if you use tactile and kinetic clues. Ask children to feel the position of the tongue, toward the front of the mouth, as they say /n/. Then ask them to say /g/ and feel the position of the tongue, way back in the mouth. Continue by having them say /n/, pulling the tongue way back into the /g/ position while making the /n/ sound. Explain that this is another sound, like /n/ and /m/, that reverberates through the nose. You can't make these sounds if you have a stuffy nose.

Use a gong, a triangle rhythm instrument, or other metal object that will make the same sound. Ring it; the sound will carry for a long time. When the sound disappears, ask children to do the same with the *ng* sound, taking a big breath and seeing how long they can continue the sound. Make the sound again and lead children in writing the two letters in the air and making the sound at the same time.

Give each child a sheet of newsprint and a black crayon or soft-lead pencil. Demonstrate how to fold the paper and number the pages to make a book. Then dictate sentences with *ng* and have children write a sentence on each page.

> dot can sing.
> bang! bang!
> it rang. (or, it is ringing.)
> it is ping pong.
> Ask children to illustrate their sentences.

Check Point

While children are drawing, go from child to child and ask each child to read the sentences back to you. Help children decode by showing them how to run their finger under the words slowly, from left to right, saying each sound.

Record individual performance on the Progress Checklist.

Extended Activities

1. Give each child a large sheet of newsprint and crayons. Display Character Cards 14-21. Have children draw each of the farm animals and then finish their picture to show things that happened at the farm in the stories.

UNIT 5

itl AND *hamilton hound*

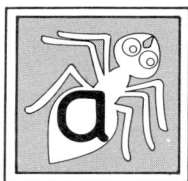

rticles *a* and *the* and digraphs *th* (voiced and unvoiced), *ch*, and *sh* are introduced in this unit. These frequently used words and digraphs are needed early in children's independent writing. In addition, numerals 6 through 10 are introduced in Lesson 44.

Some students may be beginning to label their pictures with invented spellings. If a child, for example, draws a picture of two cars bumping into each other and labels the picture *u rec*, that's cause for celebration! The child has learned to listen to the sounds in spoken words. The child knows that speech sounds are represented by certain letters and understands left-to-right order. Invented spelling is a major milestone, and children who do this should be praised. (See "Spelling" and "Original Composition" in *Writing Is Child's Play*.) Sharing information about the importance of invented spelling with parents will discourage them from trying to impose dictionary spelling on the children.

Invented spelling should be accepted until children are reading at about beginning second-grade level and have mastered alphabet order enough to use a dictionary. Once children learn to use the dictionary, they can become independent spellers as well as independent writers. Independent writing with invented spelling comes first.

Once a spelling pattern has been taught, however, children can be expected to apply the rule. For example, until children are taught the double *ll* pattern at the end of words, *tel* is acceptable for *tell*. Until the *aw* pattern is taught, "I *so* the jac rabbit" should be accepted. (Simple rules for teaching spelling to beginners are included in Appendix B of *Writing Is Child's Play*.)

Objective To recognize the word *a*, to pronounce the word (/uh/), and to write the word correctly.

Understandings Like the word *to*, the word *a* is needed early for independent writing. If it is taught as the alphabet name for the letter, children's later reading is less fluent. Most American-English speakers do not say this word with the long *a* sound, as in its alphabet name, except for special emphasis. Its pronunciation should be as close to natural speech as possible—/uh/ cat rather than ā cat.

Materials

itl puppet
Character Cards 1, 6, 13, 17
black writing crayons, one per child
crayons
newsprint—one 12″ x 15″ sheet per child

Story

Display the character cards as you tell the story.

hamilton finds anny

itl and *ed* had left the farm and were hiking through the meadow.

"Here comes *hamilton* following us!" said *ed*.

"He's always running away from the farm," said *itl*. "We'd better take him with us, or he'll get lost."

hamilton ran ahead of them. He was barking near a big rock. They heard a noise like this: "/uh/ /uh/ /uh/."

"That sounds like *uggy*," said *itl*. "He must be lost. He never goes this far from the farm." When they got to the rock it wasn't *uggy* after all. It was *anny* with a big rock on top of her.

"What happened, *anny*?" asked *ed*.

"I was practicing my weight lifting," she said. "But I guess this rock is too heavy for me. I can't get it off my chest. I can hardly breathe, /uh/ /uh/ /uh/."

itl and *ed* pushed and tugged. *hamilton* helped, too. Finally they pulled the rock off *anny*.

"Oh, thank you," she said. "I was all alone out here. I thought no one would ever hear me calling for help. I'll be more careful next time. I think I need a nap now."

"Good-bye, *anny*," said *itl*. "I'm on my way to take *ed* back to the zoo. I'll stop in to see you on my way home."

Activity

Give children newsprint and black crayons. Demonstrate how to fold the newsprint to make a four-page book. (See Activity in Lesson 13.) If children know how to make all the letters in their name correctly, have them write their name in the *GO* corner on the front of their book; if not, have them write their initials. Have them number the pages from 1 to 4.

Ask children to make the sound *anny* made in this story. Make the sound together several times. Then recall that in the story *anny* was all by herself when she was stuck under the rock. Explain that when we say /uh/ all by itself—not in a word with other sounds—we use *anny*'s letter, and if we see *anny*'s letter all by itself, we pronounce it /uh/. Explain that the word *a* means *one*. Give examples, such as *a boy, a girl, a teacher, a banana*. Then ask children to suggest other examples.

For each page of their book, dictate a phrase or sentence that includes the word *a*. Ask children to repeat each sentence before writing it. If necessary, remind children to use periods.

Suggested phrases or sentences:

it is a red hat.
a bug is in a can.
a dog is lost.
it is a big bed.
rub a dub dub three men in a tub. (Tell children to write the numeral 3.)

Following the dictation, tell children to read the sentences to themselves and then to illustrate them.

Check Point

While children are illustrating their sentences, go from child to child to see if they are writing the word correctly. Help children read what they have written by showing them how to run their finger under each letter and say each sound.

Record individual performance on the Progress Checklist.

Extended Activities

1. Look for *anny*'s letter in printed materials. Give children books or magazines and tell them to look for *anny*'s letter all by itself—not in other words. When children find *anny* all alone in print, tell them to make her /uh/ noise.

LESSON 40

Objective To recognize the voiced digraph *th*, to say its sound, as in *this*, and to write *th* in words.

Understandings The digraph *th* represents two sounds, the voiced *th* as in *this*, and the unvoiced *th* as in *thin*. The voiced *th*, is five times more frequent than the unvoiced in English (Dewey 1970). It appears ten times in the 100 most commonly used words in primary storybooks (*the, that, they, there, then, them, this, mother, other, father*). The unvoiced *th* appears only once in these words, in the word *thing*.

Materials

itl puppet
Activity Sheet 31, one copy per child
Character Cards 1, 2, 13, 17
black writing crayons, one per child

Story

Display the character cards as you tell the story.

til and hamilton

itl and *ed* left *anny* and started toward the zoo again. *hamilton* hound ran on ahead with his tongue hanging out "/h//h//h/."

After they had walked for a while, *ed* said to *itl*, "I hear a strange noise. It might be some dangerous wild animal. We'd better be careful."

They went ahead as quietly as they could toward the noise. It sounded like this: "/th//th//th/ (Vibrate the sound.)."

They rounded a bend in the path and there was *hamilton* making that strange sound! He had never seen a turtle before. There was nothing like that back at the farm! He was standing next to *til* and trying to growl with his tongue still out. The only sound he could make was "/th//th//th/."

"Stop it, *hamilton*!" yelled *itl*. "*til*'s our friend!" When *hamilton* heard *itl* say that, he slowly walked toward *til* and started wagging his tail.

Activity

Distribute Activity Sheet 31 and black crayons. Tell children to draw *til* and *hamilton* around their letters and then to write the two letters in the talking balloon. You may want to use the sequenced drawings of *til* and *hamilton* in Lessons 8 and 33 to demonstrate the steps. Ask children to say the sound *hamilton* made when he saw *til*.

When the drawings are completed, dictate the following sentences and have children write them below the picture. Teach children how to make a question mark by drawing one on the board and explaining that this sign means that the

154

sentence is asking a question. Trace the question mark on the board, explaining that it starts like a 2, but that the line at the bottom is a standing line and there is a dot on the bottom.

> is this *itl?*
> no it is *til.*
> that is a dog.

Check Point

Ask each child to make the new sound and to write the two letters that make the sound. Then ask individual children to read the sentences on Activity Sheet 31 back to you.

Record individual performance on the Progress Checklist.

Extended Activities

1. Give children newsprint and soft-lead pencils or writing crayons. Dictate sentences with *this, that, then, them.* For example, "is that mom? that is dad." Ask children to illustrate their sentences.

LESSON 41

Objective To recognize the word *the*, to say the word with the unvoiced *schwa* sound for *e* (thuh), and to write *the* correctly.

Understandings The word *the* appears in printed material more often than any other word, and twice as often as the second most frequently used word, *to*. It should be taught early in any writing or reading program. *The* is pronounced far more frequently with the unstressed *uh* sound than with the long *e* sound; thus /thuh/ should be taught first. After this lesson, children should be expected to write *the* instead of *thu* in their original compositions.

Materials

> *itl* puppet
> Activity Sheet 32, one copy per child
> Character Cards 1, 2, 13, 17
> black writing crayons, one per child

Story

Display Character Cards 2, 17, and 13 in a row to form the word *the* as you tell the story.

til, hamilton, and ed

hamilton still wasn't sure that *til* was a friend. Whenever he looked at her, he'd turn away and make that funny sound with his tongue hanging out: "/th/ /th/ /th/."

 ed was getting so tired of walking and of chasing *hamilton* that he was ready to fall asleep. He stood next to *hamilton* to rest.

 til and *hamilton* and *ed* were standing in a row. *til* was listening to her watch, "/t/ /t/ /t/," *hamilton* was panting, "/h/ /h/ /h/," and *ed* was still trying to catch his breath, "/uh/ /uh/ /uh/."

 itl laughed. "When you three stand in a row and make those noises, you make a word. You're making the word *the!*" he said.

Activity

Distribute Activity Sheet 32 and black crayons. Tell children to make the noise *hamilton* makes when he looks at *til* and to write the two letters for that sound in *hamilton*'s talking balloon. Then tell them to write *ed*'s letter in his talking balloon as they make the sound *ed* made in this story.

 Ask children to draw each animal around its own letter and then to write the word *the* below the pictures. The sequenced drawings of each letter animal in Lessons 8, 26, and 33 may be used to demonstrate the steps.

 When the drawings are completed, dictate this sentence for children to write on the activity sheet: *ed* is mad at the dog.

Check Point

Ask each child to say the new word and to write *the* for you.
Record individual performance on the Progress Checklist.

Extended Activities

1. Make Look-and-Do strips for the word *the* and use the word in the Hop-Spell game.

2. Teach the hand sign for the word *the*.

3. Choose volunteers to play *itl*, *til*, *ed*, and *hamilton*. Have them replay the story as you retell it or dramatize it using their own words.

4. Give the children newsprint and soft-lead pencils or writing crayons. Use *the* in dictation exercises. For example:

> *the* bag is big.
> is an ant big?
> *the* plant is hot.
> *itl* is mad at *hamilton*. (Dictate ham-il-ton in
> three separate syllables.)

5. Have children look for the word *the* in books or other printed material.

LESSON 42

Objective To recognize the digraph *ch*, to say its sound, as in *itch*, and to write *ch* in words.

Understandings This speech sound is produced the same way as the /j/ sound in English. The difference is that the /ch/ is not voiced and the /j/ is.

Spanish-speaking children will have no problem with it because it is a common sound in their home language (*muchacho*), and the spelling is identical.

Materials

> *itl* puppet
> Activity Sheet 33, one per child
> Character Cards 1, 5, 13, 17
> black writing crayons, one per child
> crayons
> newsprint—one large, easel-sized sheet
> black, felt-tipped pen

Story

Display the character cards as you tell the story.

cat and hamilton

itl and *ed* said good-bye to *til* and continued on their way to the zoo. *ed* was eager to get home to show the other elephants that he could write letters. *hamilton* was still with them.

hamilton ran on ahead of *itl* and *ed*, sniffing at everything because it was new to him. He had never been away from the farm before. Pretty soon, they heard *hamilton* sneezing and sneezing as he ran: "/ch/ /ch/ /ch/."

When they caught up with *hamilton*, *itl* laughed. "Look, *ed*. He was sniffing at *cat*. Some caterpillar fuzz got in his nose and made him sneeze. *hamilton*! Leave *cat* alone! He's our friend!" *itl* called.

"I'm glad you fellows came along," said *cat*. "That big hound dog practically blew me away!" *hamilton* kept sneezing: "/ch/ /ch/ /ch/."

Activity

Write a large *ch* on newsprint and ask children to make the sound. Tell children that to make this speech sound their tongue is in the same position as for the /t/ sound. Have them feel how the tongue pushes forward on the roof of the mouth. Then tell them to make the /j/ sound and feel the difference in the throat.

Distribute Activity Sheet 33 and black crayons. Ask children to make the /ch/ sound and to write the two letters for that sound in *hamilton*'s talking balloon.

Tell children to draw each animal character around its letter and to color the animals. The sequenced drawings of *cat* and *hamilton*, in Lessons 15 and 33, may be used to demonstrate the steps. Then dictate this sentence for children to write below their drawing: the dog has a chin.

Check Point

Ask each child to make the new sound and to write the two letters.
Record individual performance on the Progress Checklist.

Extended Activities

1. Add the digraph *ch* to your Look-and-Do strips.

2. Choose volunteers to replay the story as you retell it, or to dramatize it using their own words.

3. Give children newsprint and soft-lead pencils or black crayons. Dictate words, phrases, and sentences. Have children repeat each statement aloud and then write it. When you are through dictating, ask children to read the sentences aloud to themselves and then to illustrate them.

> the man can *chop*.
> a *chest* has lungs in it.
> a *chip* is in the bag.
> the pig has a *chin* in the dust.

4. If you are using the *itl Early Writing Program* as a remedial writing and spelling program with children beyond kindergarten, this would be a good time to point out this primary spelling rule: When this speech sound is preceded by a short-vowel sound we often add a *t* (*catch, itch*).

LESSON 43

Objective To recognize the digraph *sh*, to say its sound, and to write *sh* in words.

Understandings Children are familiar with this sound in words and with the sound as a signal for quiet. Children who lisp may need special help in reproducing it. The teeth are closed as with /s/ to keep the tongue back.

Materials

itl puppet

Activity Sheet 34, one per child

Character Cards 1, 11, 13, 17

black writing crayons, one per child

crayons

newsprint—one large, easel-sized sheet

black, felt-tipped pen

Story

Display the character cards as you tell the story.

sissy and hamilton

itl and *ed* left *cat* in the meadow. He was busy combing his fuzz. It was all tangled after *hamilton*'s big sneezes.

"That *hamilton!*" said *itl.* "What will he do next?"

"Puppies are a bother," said *ed.* "I wish he'd stop getting into trouble so we could go on to the zoo. How much further is it, *itl?*"

"We have to go around the pond and through the forest," *itl* answered. "The zoo is on the other side of the forest. Maybe we'll see *olly* and *fred* and *sissy* again. They live at the pond."

"Maybe I can wade in the water and cool off my feet!" *ed* said.

All of a sudden they saw *hamilton* up ahead. He was standing very still and staring at something. When they got to the edge of the pond they saw that *hamilton* was standing next to *sissy.* She was taking a nap.

itl whispered to *hamilton,* "/sh//shhhhhhhhh/. Leave her alone, *hamilton.* It's not polite to wake creatures when they're sleeping. Let's be quiet. /shhhhhhhhhh/."

Activity

Write a large *sh* on newsprint and ask children to make the sound that *itl* made in the story. Tell children to feel the position of the tongue for this sound: It is pulled back slightly in the mouth and flattened. Ask them to make the /s/ sound and then the /sh/ sound to feel the different tongue positions. Point out that the lips are more protruded for /sh/. Remind children to keep their teeth closed so that their tongue won't peep out.

Distribute Activity Sheet 34 and black crayons. Tell children to draw each animal around its letter and then to write *sh* in the talking balloon. The sequenced drawings of *sissy* and *hamilton* in Lessons 21 and 33 may be used to demonstrate the steps. Have them write *sh* below the pictures several times, each time saying the new sound.

Check Point

Ask each child to make the new sound and to write the two letters.

Record individual performance on the Progress Checklist.

Extended Activities

1. Add the digraph *sh* to your Look-and-Do strips.

2. Choose volunteers to play *itl, hamilton, ed,* and *sissy.* Have them replay the story as you retell it or dramatize it using their own words.

3. Use a card with *sh* written on it as a signal for children to be quiet.

4. Give children newsprint and soft-lead pencils or black crayons. Dictate sentences that have *sh* in words, having children repeat each sentence and then write it. Tell children to read the sentences to themselves and then to illustrate them.

the fish is in the can.
it is a big shop.
it is a shin. it is a chin.
it is open. shut it.

LESSON 44

Objective To recognize and write the numerals 6-10.

Understandings Except for *7*, these numerals start on the right side and move toward the left (the same curve as for *c, a, d, g, f, o, s*). The numeral *7* is the first symbol with a diagonal stroke taught in the *itl Early Writing Program.* Diagonals are the most difficult writing strokes to make because they move in two directions at once, either up or down and to the left or right.

Children reverse numerals more often than they reverse letters. One reason for this is that children often try to copy numbers very early. Parents often let their children continue to write numerals incorrectly without correcting them. Once these children start school, their numeral reversals have become a habit that is difficult to change. The "Mother Number" story gives children a method for remembering which way the numerals face.

Children who habitually reverse numerals are sometimes those who hesitate to cross the midline of the body, the invisible line dividing the body into two mirror images. (Review "Midline Difficulty" in *Writing Is Child's Play* for suggestions that may help children with this problem.)

Materials

 itl puppet
Activity Sheets 35 and 36, one copy of each per child
black writing crayons, one per child
crayons
newsprint—three large, easel-sized sheets
black, green, and red felt-tipped pens

Preparation

For the second part of the activity, draw a house like the one on Activity Sheet 36 in the center of a large sheet of newsprint, near the top of the sheet.

Story

Draw the rocks and numerals on newsprint as they are described in the story.

itl writes numbers

sissy was still sleeping. *itl* and *ed* sat down quietly near her to rest. *hamilton* ran off to splash in the water. *ed* picked up some little rocks and placed them in rows in the mud. He made two rows of three rocks, like this. (Draw rocks as shown):

• •
• •
• •

Then he counted them: "one, two, three, four, five, six. Three and three make six," he said. "*itl*, how do I make a six?"

"Just use your rocks to help you," said *itl*. "Start on the top, on the *STOP* side. Go all around the rocks until you come to the last one. Then curl your line over to the middle rock on the *GO* side. Be sure you touch all six rocks. It's just like *cat*'s initial, only you curl back to his tummy at the end." (Draw a *6* on the newsprint.)

6

"That's easy," said *ed*. "I can even do it without any rocks." And he did.

Then *ed* made two groups of four rocks, one on top of the other, and counted them. (Draw eight dots.)

• •
• •
• •
• •

"How do I make an eight, *itl?*" *ed* asked.

"Eight is tricky," said *itl*. "Look at *sissy* over there. Pretend you're making her initial. Now you have one rock left over. Keep on going uphill, touch that last rock, then go back to the beginning rock." (Draw an *8.*)

8

"These rocks sure help," said *ed*. "What about nine?"

"You don't need rocks for nine," said *itl*. "You already know how to write *anny*'s letter. The numeral nine is just the same except it has a longer stick. Keep it straight." (Draw a *9.*)

9

ed made a nine in the mud.

"How about ten?" asked *ed*.

"You don't need any help with that one, either," said *itl*. "It's just a stick and then a circle like *olly*. Be sure you start at the top." (Draw a *10.*)

10

"Six, eight, nine, ten. Which one did we leave out, *itl?*" *ed* asked.

"You forgot seven. That's a tricky one," said *itl*. "It starts on the *GO* side. First you make a resting line toward the *STOP* side. Then you make a sliding line back to the *GO* side." (Draw a *7*.)

Activity

Write the numerals on a sheet of newsprint as you describe the strokes. After writing each numeral, ask children to write it in the air with you. Write *6*, *8*, and *9*, the numerals that begin on the *STOP* side, first. Then write *10*. Write *7*, which starts on the *GO* side, last. Point out that the slide on the *7* stops right under the starting place.

Distribute Activity Sheet 35 and black crayons. For each numeral, have children count the dots and then write the numeral over the dots. Have children write *6*, *8*, and *9* first, then *10* and *7*.

Using the sheet of newsprint with the house drawn on it, tell this story, writing the numerals on the newsprint as they are described in the story.

This is the Number house. Mother and Father Number had ten children. The baby was one. The biggest child was ten. The others were in between. When they played together in their backyard, the big ones were always playing so rough that the little ones got knocked down. Daddy Number finally built a fence down the middle of the yard. (Draw a line down the middle of the newsprint to represent the fence.)

"Now," he said,"you little children play on the *STOP* side near the red flowers. (Draw red circles down the right side to represent flowers.)

Mother Number let the little children out one at a time. First she let baby one out. (Make a *1* near the red flowers.)

Then two, three, four and five went out. They played near the flowers. (Draw *2*, *3*, *4*, and *5* in order, toward the red flowers.)

Then Mother Number let six out. She played near the grass on the other side of the fence. (Draw some green grass on the left side of the paper. Then draw *6* near the left side.)

Seven couldn't go out because he hadn't made his bed. The other big numbers went out and played near the grass. (Leaving room in the sequence for *7*, write *8*, *9*, and *10* near the left side.)

When seven had made his bed, Mother Number let him go outside. Mother reminded seven to play near the grass. (Write *7* in the sequence.)

Distribute Activity Sheet 36. Repeat the story, having children write the numerals as the story is told.

Check Point

Ask each child to write the numerals *1-10* without copying them.

Record individual performance on the Progress Checklist.

Extended Activities

1. Send home Parent Letter 10.

LESSON 45

Objective To recognize the unvoiced digraph *th*, as in *bath*, and to distinguish it from the voiced digraph *th*, as in *this*.

Understandings This speech sound is much less frequent in English than the voiced /th/. Children will confuse the unvoiced *th* sound with the /f/ sound if they try to discriminate it only by ear. They need to *feel* how these sounds are made in the mouth and then to *see* your face when you are dictating words to them. Children who are substituting /f/ for /th/ in their speech (one, two, free) may have a hard time discriminating these two sounds.

Materials

itl puppet
Character Cards 1, 2, 10, 13, 17
black writing crayons, one per child
crayons
newsprint—one 12″ x 15″ sheet per child

Story

Display the character cards as you tell the story.

hamilton's new sound

itl and *ed* were still cooling off at the pond before continuing their long walk to the zoo. *ed* sucked a lot of water up in his long trunk and showered everybody to get the mud off.

"What's that noise?" asked *itl*. "It sounds a little bit like *fred*, but *fred* is right here. He isn't making that noise."

itl turned around. It was *hamilton* again! Now what? Then they all laughed. *hamilton* had made so many new noises all afternoon that his voice wouldn't work any more.

til had come over to the pond to cool off. *hamilton* was trying to make that funny noise at her again with his tongue out. The only noise that came out was a little whisper noise like this: "/th//th//th/."

"Now maybe he'll stop bothering our friends," said *itl*. "Come on, *ed*. We'd better get started if we're ever going to get to the zoo. Good-bye, everybody."

And off they went again.

Activity

Repeat *hamilton's* new sound for children and then ask them to make the sound.

Distribute newsprint and black crayons. Show children how to fold their paper to make a book. Dictate the following sentences, telling children to write each sentence on a separate page. Remind children to watch your face so that they will know whether the sound is /f/ or /th/.

    it is a thin fish.
    the fish has a fin.
    the thing is red.
    this is the thong.

Have children illustrate their sentences and then color their drawings.

Check Point

Ask each child to make the new sound and to write the letters *th*.
    Record individual performance on the Progress Checklist.

Extended Activities

1. Choose volunteers to play *itl*, *til*, *ed*, and *hamilton*. Have them replay the story as you retell it or dramatize it using their own words.

2. Use a mirror for children who cannot discriminate between /f/ and the unvoiced /th/. Show them the two mouth positions. Whenever they make *hamilton*'s new sound, the tongue is peeking out, just like his.

6 UNIT *itl* GOES CAMPING

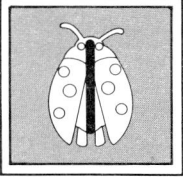

ong-vowel sounds are introduced in this unit. Vowels are the only letters whose alphabet names young children *need* to know in order to read and write efficiently. Many children may already be familiar with these sounds; some may be able to recite the alphabet or sing the alphabet song.

In addition, spelling cues for long-vowel sounds are introduced. Children learn to recognize that an *e* at the end of a word or a double vowel are often cues for a long-vowel sound. Writing and reading will make more sense to beginners if we show them that written language is a system. It is not a perfect system, like math, but a system that has rules. The rules introduced in this unit will help children solve some of the spelling-pronunciation puzzles they will encounter in writing and reading tasks.

LESSON 46

Objective To say the alphabet names for the vowels *a, e, i, o, u.*

Understandings Children already have been introduced to the major sounds for these letters—their more frequently used short-vowel sounds. They have learned the correct formation for these letters. They have already been introduced to the long *o* in the stories about the octopus brothers in Unit 3. This lesson teaches children the long-vowel sounds for *a, e, i,* and *u.*

Materials

   itl puppet
   Character Cards 1, 6, 12, 13, 14
   black writing crayons, one per child
   crayons
   newsprint—one 12″ x 15″ sheet per child
   black, felt-tipped pen

Story

   Display the character cards as you tell the story.

Alphabet letter names for anny, ed, itl, olly, and uggy

It was late afternoon. *itl* and *ed* were still on their way to the zoo. Keeping *hamilton* out of trouble had made their walk longer. While they were resting at the pond, *dotty* dalmatian had come to play in the water. She told *itl* that she would take *hamilton* back to the farm so he wouldn't get lost.

   As *itl* and *ed* were walking through the forest, they heard a voice calling, "*olly! uggy!* Look who's here! It's *itl* and *ed.*"

   "*anny!*" laughed *itl,* "What are you three doing here?"

   "Oh, we're camping," answered *anny.* "What are you two doing here?"

   "I'm taking *ed* back to the zoo. He was lost, you know."

   "Why don't you spend the night with us?" asked *olly.*

   "That's a great idea," said *itl.* "We're tired."

   That evening *olly* built a big campfire. They toasted marshmallows and made popcorn. *anny* made hot chocolate. Then *olly* made up some funny songs. They all sang together:

   ed and *itl* went to the farm . . . ă ĕ ĭ ŏ ŭ (short-vowel sounds),
   And on the farm they saw a rooster . . . *r r r r r,*
   With an *r r* here, and an *r r* there,
   Here an *r,* there an *r,* everywhere an *r r,*
   ed and *itl* went to the farm . . . ă ĕ ĭ ŏ ŭ.

Then they all helped *anny* clean up the dishes and got ready for bed.

   olly let *itl* and *ed* use his sleeping bag. He climbed into the water bucket to sleep. *olly* was singing quietly to himself, ŏ ô ō ōō ŏŏ . . . ŏ ô ō ōō ŏŏ (the speech sounds heard in *ŏn, ôff, nō, zōō, gŏŏd*). "What are you singing, *olly?*" asked *itl.* "Teach it to us."

"Oh, that's easy," laughed *olly.* "You just keep your mouth round, but you start with it open as wide as you can; then you just keep making it smaller and smaller. You can use my letter for all those sounds. The middle-sized mouth is my special alphabet name, *ō.*"

"*ā* is my alphabet name," said *anny.* "Mine is easy to remember because it comes first when you sing the alphabet song."

"Mine is easy to remember, too," said *itl.* "My alphabet name is *ı.* It's the word I use when I talk about myself."

"I know mine, too," said *ed.* "I just think about my littlest sister back at the zoo. Her name is *eedy.* Her name starts with the same letter but a different sound. My alphabet name is *ē.*"

They all sat up and looked at *uggy* who was being very quiet. "What's your alphabet name, *uggy?*" asked *ed.*

uggy looked very sad. "I don't know. I can't remember names at all. I just call everybody, 'hey, you.'"

The other animals all laughed and laughed.

"I don't think it's funny," said *uggy.* "It's not polite to laugh at animals when it's hard for them to learn to do something."

"We're not laughing at you," said *itl.* "We're laughing because you just said your alphabet name. It's the easiest of all. All you have to remember is to say, 'hey, you!' Your alphabet name is *ū.*"

Then *uggy* laughed too. "I can remember that! My alphabet name is *ū.*"

"Let's sing our silly song with our alphabet names," said *olly.* "Let's sing about *uggy.*" And they did, like this:

ed and *itl* went to the farm . . . *ā ē ı̄ ō ū* (long-vowel
sounds),
And on the farm they saw a duck . . . *ū ū ū ū ū* (long-vowel
sound),
With a *ū ū* here, and a *ū ū* there,
Here a *ū*, there a *ū*, everywhere a *ū ū*,
ed and *itl* went to the farm . . . *ā ē ı̄ ō ū.*

Activity

Give each child newsprint and a black crayon. Demonstrate folding a sheet of newsprint to make a book and have children fold their paper. (See Lesson 13.) Remind them that books open on the *STOP* side. Go from child to child checking book position; emphasize the word *right*, associating it with the *STOP* side. By this time the majority of your group can probably write their first name, instead of their initials, on the cover. Help children individually if they have letters in their names that have not been introduced (*k y w x v z*).

Tell children to number their book pages from 1 to 4 and then to turn back to the cover. Dictate the alphabet names for *a, e, i, o,* and *u,* telling children to write all these letters on the cover. Tell them to write the letters big so that they can turn them into animal pictures later.

For each of the other pages, dictate common single-syllable words ending in long vowels. (The letter *a* does not fit this long-vowel pattern: *ha ha, mama, papa.*)

Page 2	Page 3	Page 4
me	hi	so
he		go
be		no
she		ho ho

Tell children to illustrate at least one of the words on each page and then to draw the animals around the letters on the cover.

Check Point

While children are drawing and coloring, go from child to child and point to the letters on the cover of the book as you ask each child to say the alphabet names of these five letters. Point to the letters in random order so they are not just reciting a pattern they've heard.

Record individual performance on the Progress Checklist.

Extended Activities

1. Give children newsprint and soft-lead pencils or writing crayons. Make a chart to show how a vowel changes its sound when it changes its position. Dictate the words on the chart, asking children to repeat each word and then to write it.

on	no
og	go
eh	he
ih	hi
em	me

2. Ask children what *name* people say when they are talking about themselves. (*I*) Write a capital *I* on the board and point out that we write that name—*I*—with a capital letter, the same way we write our initials.

Give children a sheet of newsprint and a pencil. Dictate the sentence "I am _____." and tell children to fill in their own name. Help any children who have trouble writing their name.

Have children use crayons to draw a self-portrait on the paper.

LESSON 47

Objective To recognize that an *e* at the end of a word is often a cue for a long-vowel sound.

Understandings You may want to postpone this lesson until the entire alphabet has been taught. Young children need to know, however, that the placement of letters in a word will often tell them how to say the word.

Once a rule has been taught, give children time to practice it before correcting mistakes. For example, a toddler shows a sign of remarkable progress in spoken language when he says "bringed," "throwed," or "writed." The child has acquired an important rule that is regularly applied in English for past-tense verb endings. That this child has applied it to irregular verbs is of little concern. The regularities of language are mastered before the irregularities. Similarly, if a young child writes *ete* for *eat,* or *rede* for *read,* praise the use of a cue to indicate a special sound. See the "Primary Spelling Rules," Appendix B, in *Writing Is Child's Play.*

Materials

itl puppet
Character Cards 1, 6, 12, 13, 14
black writing crayons, one per child
newsprint—one 12″ x 15″ sheet per child
word cards (See *Preparation.*)

Preparation

For the story, prepare individual word cards for the words *at, ate, can, cane, cut, cute, dim, dime, not, note.* Write the words in large black letters on construction paper or tagboard. For *Check Point,* prepare word cards for the words *game, hide, home, made, nose.*

Story

Display the character cards and word cards as you present the story. Each time a word is displayed, ask children to read it.

ed helps make words
After a big camp breakfast, *anny, ed, itl, olly,* and *uggy* were still singing the farm song using their last names, *a, e, i, o, u.*

"Sing about me," said *ed.* (Invite the children to sing along.)

ed and *itl* went to the farm, *a, e, i, o, u,*
and on the farm they saw an elephant, *ee ee ee ee ee.*
With an *ee ee* here, and an *ee ee* there,
Here an *ee,* there an *ee,* everywhere an *ee ee,*
ed and *itl* went to the farm, *a, e, i, o, u.*

anny looked confused. "If I'm going to be an astronaut," she said, "I'll have to learn to write and read. How do we know when to say our regular name and when to use our last name, like *a, e, i, o, u?*"

"That's not too easy," said *itl.* "It's kind of like a puzzle. You have to know how to use the clues. I'll show you. But we'll need to work together on it."

"Let me help," said *ed.*

"OK," said *itl.* "You can be first. I'll write a word here on the ground." He wrote *can.* (Display word card.)

"Now, *ed,*" he said. "Stand at the end of the letter to remind *anny* to say her alphabet name in the word."

ed stood on the end like this. (Use the *ed* character card with *can* and then show the *cane* card.)

"I get it now," laughed *anny.* "Now it says *cane,* like a *candy cane. ed* stood on the end to remind me to say my alphabet name, *a.*"

Then *ed* helped them turn
at into *ate*
not into *note*
cut into *cute*
dim into *dime*

Activity

Distribute newsprint and black crayons. Dictate sentences for children to write that include words where a final, silent *e* signals the use of a long-vowel sound.
the *pin* is in the *pine.* I *ate* it at *home.*
the *cub* is on the *cube.* it is *not* a *note.*
Tell children to illustrate their sentences.

Check Point

While children are drawing, go from child to child showing other words with the silent *e* pattern. Ask individual children to read the words aloud.
nose game hide
home made
Record individual performance on the Progress Checklist.

Extended Activities

1. Show children how to put the macron line above vowels (¯) to indicate the long sound. This is an easier task for beginners than adding an extra vowel. It does, however, make young children aware of the need to cue their writing in some way so others may read it. Write *a, e, i, o, u* three times on the chalkboard. Ask a child to come to the board. Say *a* and ask the child to repeat the sound, to find the letter, and to draw a line above it. Repeat with other children.

2. Demonstrate to children why we call some vowels short and some long. Explain that a short vowel makes a single speech sound (*ă, ĕ, ĭ, ŏ, ŭ*) and that when we say the name sound for *a, i, o,* or *u,* we make *two* speech sounds. Use a mirror to show children that their mouth changes its position from *eh* to *ee* when they say the alphabet name for the letter *a.* The letter *i* is pronounced with two sounds, *ah, ee.* The mouth shrinks for the letter *o* from *oh* to *oo.* The letter *u*'s name is *ee-oo.* Obviously, two sounds are longer than one sound, so we call these sounds long. The letter *e* is the exception. Its name is only one sound, *ee.*

LESSON 48

Objective To recognize that double-vowel patterns are often cues for a long-vowel sound.

Understandings If some kindergarten children are beginning to try to figure out words in storybooks, you will make their task easier if you give them some useful clues for variant vowel sounds. You may want to use this lesson only with those children. If you are using the *itl Early Writing Program* with first-grade or older children, they will need to understand and use common double-vowel patterns. If they are given some simple rules, the difficult written English language patterns can begin to make some sense to them. Vowel patterns in English are extremely variant. It makes sense to begin teaching with the most common patterns. The vowel pattern *ea*, for example, represents the long-vowel sound for *e* (*eat*) more than three times as often as it represents its short sound, as in *bread.* It represents the sound in *eat* almost six times more frequently than the *a* sound, as in *great* (Dewey 1970).

Deciding which long-vowel spelling pattern to use is much too difficult for beginners (*road* or *rode*, for example). Young children, however, can learn that when writing independently, they must give the reader some cue to indicate when they are using a long-vowel sound. Often in English that cue is a second vowel.

The only speech *sound* not yet introduced is the sound for the letter *v.* All other sounds in the next unit have been introduced with other letters. Thus children can substitute *c* for *k*, *ee* for *y*, and *oo* for *w* in their independent writing at this stage. They have been introduced to all the sounds they use in their everyday speech. They can therefore record anything they can say. Give special help, of course, to any child who needs the sound for *v* in independent composition.

Materials

> *itl* puppet
> Character Cards 1, 6, 12, 13, 14
> black writing crayons, one per child
> crayons
> newsprint—one 12″ x 15″ sheet per child
> black, felt-tipped pen
> word cards (See *Preparation.*)

Preparation

For the story, prepare the following word cards with the second vowel missing: *re_d, co_t, blu_, ra_n, gre_n.* Write the words in large black letters on construction paper or tagboard.

Story

Display the character cards and word cards as you present the story. Each time a word is displayed, ask children to read it.

anny, ed, itl, olly and uggy help each other

itl and *ed* were still making up words with the alphabet name sounds, *a, e, i, o, u.*

"*ed* always gets to be the helper," said *anny.* "Let me try. I can help, too."
itl wrote this word in the forest dirt. (Display the word card *re_d.*)

anny squeezed in next to *ed*'s letter. (Write the letter *a* on the blank.)
"Good," said *itl.* "You are a good helper."

"I get it," said *ed.* "Now my word says *read.*"
Then *itl* wrote, *co_t.* (Display the word card.)

anny squeezed in next to *olly*'s letter. (Add the missing vowel.)
"I get it now," said *olly.* "My word says *coat. anny* helped me say my alphabet name in that word."

"I think I'm getting it now," said *uggy.* "The first one you come to says its alphabet name. That's the noisy one. The other one doesn't make any noise. It just helps. Do one with my letter. You help me, *ed.*" *itl* wrote *blu_.*

Then *ed* stood after *uggy* at the end. (Add the missing vowel.)
"I get it. I get it!" yelled *uggy.* "It's a color. It says *blue.*"

"Watch me help now," said *itl.* First he wrote *ra_n.* Then he squeezed in after *anny*'s letter. (Add the *i.*) "What am I now?" *itl* asked.

"I know. It's *rain,*" smiled *anny.* "I think I'm really going to be an astronaut now. I can read hard words."

"I can even help myself now," said *ed.* "Watch." He wrote *gre_n.*
Then he squeezed in next to his own letter. (Add the *e.*) "See, I made *green.*"

Activity

Distribute newsprint and black crayons. Show children how to fold their paper into a book. (See Lesson 13.) Then tell children to number the pages from 1 to 4.

Present the words *green, blue, three, four,* in the following manner:
• Write the word on the board.
• Ask children to read the word and then to write it in the air.
• Erase the word and ask children to write it on a page in their book from memory; tell them to write each word on a separate page.

When children have written the words, have them illustrate each word (something green, something blue, three things, four things).

Check Point

Dictate the four words—*green, blue, three, four*—and have children write them without copying them.

Record individual performance on the Progress Checklist.

Extended Activities

1. Give children newsprint and black crayons. Repeat the lesson activity using words such as *red, ten, six, seven, five, nine.*

UNIT 7

itl
AT THE ZOO

ight-curve letters *y* and *w* and lowercase letters that have diagonal strokes—*k*, *v*, *x*, and *z*—are introduced in this unit. Diagonal lines are the hardest letter strokes for children to make; a diagonal moves in two directions at the same time, up or down *and* left or right. Writing these lowercase letters with diagonal lines will prepare students for learning to write capital letters, which have many more diagonal strokes.

Spelling rules to help children use *c* and *k* correctly in spelled words are also included in this unit.

LESSON 49

Objective To recognize the letter *k*, to say its speech sound, and to write the letter correctly.

Understandings This is not a new speech sound for students; it is a new letter for the same sound made by *cat* caterpillar.

Letters made with diagonal lines going in different directions are the hardest letters to make. The letter *k*, made with two different diagonals, is exceptionally difficult. The ability to make this "arrow" point does not normally develop until age six-and-a-half. The basic continuous-line cursive form for the *k* has only one diagonal and can be learned earlier. The beginning strokes for this *k* are the same as for the letter *p*—a vertical stroke followed by a right curve.

Materials

itl puppet

Audiocassette, Side 2, "*kelly kangaroo*"

Character Cards 1, 13, 22

my itl book Activity 21, one per child

black writing crayons, one per child

crayons

newsprint—one large, easel-sized sheet

black, felt-tipped pen

Story

Display the character cards as you either tell the story or play the recording.

kelly kangaroo

itl and *ed* continued their long walk to the zoo. *ed* was getting more and more excited. He could hardly wait to show the elephants that he could write letters!

"Well, we're almost there," said *ed*. "Can you hear those zoo noises, *itl*? I told you it was just like the noise at the farm."

itl listened very carefully.

"Listen, *ed*," he said. "That's *cat* caterpillar's sound. How did he get to the zoo before us?"

They heard: "c-c-c-c."

As soon as *itl* and *ed* were inside the zoo, they went to the spot the noise was coming from. There they found a big cloud of dust.

itl called, "*cat*, is that you in there in all that dust?"

A large, furry face peered out of the cloud. "I'm in here," said a voice, "and I'm no cat! I'm *kelly* kangaroo. And I'm choking to death from all this dust. c-c-c-c!"

"Why don't you come out of there if the dust bothers you so much?" *itl* asked her.

"Because I make the dust with my hopping," she wheezed. "Every time I try to hop out of one cloud of dust I make a new one. c-c-c-c-!"

itl suggested that *kelly* sit down and wait for the dust to settle, which she did.

"Look, *itl*," *ed* said. "I think I can make *kelly*'s letter." Holding a stick in his trunk, he made a long stick line, a round hump, and a slidy line to the ground.

itl had no more than admired *ed*'s work, when the letter disappeared.

"That's funny," said *ed*, and he wrote the letter again. The same thing happened. "Am I magic?" wondered *ed*.

Then *itl* laughed. "Now I see what's happening," he said. "It's *kelly*'s dust cloud. The dust keeps falling and filling in the lines you make in the dirt."

ed laughed too. "I thought it was too much, to learn to write and do magic all in the same day," he said.

Activity

Write the letter *k* in the air, describing each stroke: "Start with a long stick line. Go back about halfway up the stick, make a round bump like the top of *piggy*'s initial, and then make a slidy line down to the ground." Ask the children to say the sound as they write the letter in the air. Repeat several times.

Distribute the tear-out section of *my itl book* Activity 21. Demonstrate the steps in drawing *kelly* on a large sheet of newsprint and have children complete their drawing.

Draw *kelly*'s letter, head, body, tail, and feet as shown.

Then add the talking balloon and write *kelly*'s letter in it as you say the sound.

Tell children to write several of *kelly*'s letter below the picture, making the sound as they write. Then have them color *kelly*.

Check Point ·

As children are completing their drawing, ask each child to make the new sound and to write the letter.

Record individual performance on the Progress Checklist.

Extended Activities

1. Distribute *my itl books* and crayons. Have children turn to page 21, write *kelly*'s letter in the talking balloon as they say the letter, and color *kelly*.

2. Distribute Activity Sheet 37, crayons, and scissors. Have children color and cut out *kelly* kangaroo. Then help them attach their cutout to a folded strip of construction paper or a wooden stick, to make a stick puppet. The puppets may be used to enact the story.

3. Add the new sound and letter to the activities you've already established: Tello game, Look-and-Do strips, feely boxes, magnetic letters, Hop-Spell game.

4. Teach children the hand sign for the letter *k*.

5. Have children form the letter *k* with their body, saying the sound as they make the letter.

6. Choose several children to replay the story, either pantomiming it or dramatizing it using their own words.

7. Play "Solo Kickball." Materials: soccer ball, goals or goal lines. On the playground, make goal lines at either end of your playing area (up to forty feet apart for five-year-olds). Using a soccer ball, each child starts at one goal line and kicks the ball over the other goal line, running after it as it moves ahead and kicking it as many times as necessary. Then the child reverses the path and kicks the ball back to the starting line. This can be a competitive game, like a relay, if each pair of contestants is fairly equal in skills. This activity helps to develop coordination. Observe which foot each child seems to prefer for kicking; it may be different from the dominant hand for writing and drawing. Sometimes mixed dominance makes it harder to learn left and right tasks like writing. If necessary, give these children more individual help in whole-body movement to help develop left and right awareness. For example, you might sing and play "Looby-Loo" with all children facing the same way.

8. Send home Parent Letter 11.

Objective To use the letters *c* and *k* correctly in spelled words: *c* before *a, o,* and *u* and *k* before *i* and *e.*

Understandings The letter *k* appeared early in the development of the alphabet. The roman alphabet used *c, k,* and *q* for similar speech sounds. The *k* was then dropped, until after the Norman conquest of England. The Norman-French used *c* for the /s/ sound, as do modern French and Spanish. When the Normans tried to pronounce Anglo-Saxon words like *cyng* and *cyn* (*king* and *kin*), they ran into a decoding problem, confusing these words with *sing* and *sin.* They solved their problem by bringing back the old roman letter *k* before the vowel letters *i, e,* and *y* to indicate the /k/ sound rather than the /s/ sound. The letter *k* serves the same purpose in modern written English.

Materials

    itl puppet
    Character Cards 1, 5, 6, 12, 13, 14, 22
    crayons
    newsprint—one 12″ x 15″ sheet per child
    pencils, one per child

Story

Display the character cards as you tell the story.

kelly and cat

ed had just finished making *kelly* kangaroo's letter in the dust at the zoo. He made *cat* caterpillar's letter right next to it.

    "*itl*," he said, "how do we know which of these letters to use? They both make the same sound."

    "I'm not sure," said *itl.* "But I think it works this way—think about where our friends live: *cat* lives up in the meadow near *anny,* right?"

    "Right," said *ed.*

    "That's right next to the pond where *olly* lives. Right? And it's near the farm where *uggy* lives? Right?" *itl* went on.

    "Right," said *ed.*

    "Well, you use *cat*'s letter before *anny*'s, *olly*'s, and *uggy*'s letters," *itl* said. "You and I have been to the zoo. We're here with the kangaroo. So you use *kelly*'s letter before your letter and before my letter."

    Then *itl* made up a rhyme to help *ed* remember when to use *kelly*'s letter:

    Who's at the zoo
    With the kangaroo?
    Use your head,
    It's *itl* and *ed.*

Activity

Have children repeat *itl*'s rhyme with you. Then give each child newsprint and a pencil. Dictate sentences that have *c* or *k* in the initial position in words, emphasizing the following vowel sound so children can determine whether to use *c* or *k*.

a *k*itten is a *c*at's *k*id.
the *k*id got *c*ut on the *c*ot.

Have students use crayons to illustrate the sentences.

Check Point

While children are illustrating their sentences, go from child to child to see if children have followed the spelling rule for *c* and *k*. Ask children to read their sentences to you; help them if necessary. Have children who haven't followed the rule repeat the rhyme with you. Help them discover the error and rewrite the words correctly.

Record individual performance on the Progress Checklist.

LESSON 51

Objective To use the endings *ke* and *ck* correctly.

Understandings Instead of doubling the *c* before a second syllable or word ending that begins with a vowel, the *ck* spelling pattern is used. Otherwise, we might have a tendency to decode words like *licking* (if spelled *liccing*), as *licsing*.

Very few English words, especially those found in beginning reading, end in *c*. *Picnic* and *music* are rare exceptions. The *ck* is used instead following short vowels, and the *ke* pattern following long vowels.

In *ke* endings, the *e* is there to indicate that the preceding vowel has a long-vowel sound.

Materials

itl puppet
Character Cards 1, 5, 13, 22
crayons
newsprint—one 12″ x 15″ sheet per child
pencils, one per child

Story

Display the character cards as you tell the story.

more about kelly and cat

ed was still puzzled about when to use *cat*'s letter and when to use *kelly* kangaroo's letter.

"It makes sense to use *cat* when the next letter is *anny, olly,* and *uggy* because those friends live near each other. But what do we do when a word *ends* in the /k/ sound? What do we do when there's no letter after to tell us which letter to use?"

"That's a tricky one, *ed*," said *itl*. "If a word has an *e* on the end to remind *anny, olly, uggy* or you or me to say our alphabet names, then you use *kelly*'s letter. She goes with you and me. Remember? The rest of the time, when I'm not sure, I put both letters there."

"That's a good idea," said *ed*. "Just use both *cat* and *kelly* together at the end."

Activity

Give children newsprint and pencils. Dictate the following sentences, reminding children to use *ke* if the preceding vowel says its alphabet name and to use *c* and *k* the rest of the time.

> the du*ck* is si*ck*.
> it ate the ca*ke*.
> ti*ck*-to*ck*. it is the clo*ck*.
> this is his backpa*ck*.
> I li*ke* to ba*ke*.

Ask children to illustrate their sentences.

Check Point

While children are illustrating their sentences, go from child to child to see if they have used *ke* and *ck* correctly. Help children discover their errors by reminding them that *ke* is used following letters that have their alphabet name sound and *ck* after letters that don't use the alphabet name sound. Encourage children to rewrite sentences correctly and then to read the sentences.

Record individual performance on the Progress Checklist.

Extended Activities

1. Encourage children to look for *c* and *k* in the words in children's storybooks. Tell them to check the letters before or after these letters to see if they agree with the rules you have taught.

Objective To recognize the letter *y*, to say its sound, as in *happy*, and to write the letter correctly.

Understandings In English the speech sound for the letter *y* is pronounced /ee/ four times more often than it is pronounced with the letter name for *i*. We begin, therefore, with /ee/; this sound is never pronounced *ee-uh*. The letter *y* appears as an ending sound in English five times more often than as a beginning sound (Dewey 1970). It makes sense, therefore, to introduce it to beginners in the ending position.

When this letter is taught first as /ee/, it serves as a useful tool for writing and reading. We begin by teaching it as a familiar ending (*mommy, daddy, baby, Jimmy*). We then change the letter's position (yes—*ee-es*, yellow—*ee-ellow*; yummy—*ee-um-ee*). Young children can also use this sound-symbol relationship for common diphthongs with no extra instruction (toy—*to-ee*, boy—*bo-ee*), or even for long-vowel glides (may—*ma-ee*).

Children have already been introduced to other ways to write this same speech sound in Unit 6 (*me, see, eat*). Now they need to use the letter *y* to avoid confusion between sounds. For example, it would be difficult to figure out how to pronounce the word *yes* if it were spelled *eees* or *eaes*.

In some American dialects the final *y* sounds more like *ih*. This should cause no more confusion to children than the slight difference between the *o*'s in *hot dog*.

The letter *y* is made from the foundation strokes for the cursive *y*. This letter simply takes the letter *u* and the curl of the letter *j* and combines them without lifting the writing tool. Children don't need to learn a second form for the letter *y* in later years; they simply add the strokes for joined cursive.

Materials

itl puppet
Audiocassette, Side 2, "*ysabel yak*"
Character Cards 1, 13, 23
my itl book Activity 22, one per child
black writing crayons, one per child
crayons
newsprint—one large, easel-sized sheet
black, felt-tipped pen

Story

Display the character cards as you either tell the story or play the recording.

ysabel yak
itl and *ed* left *kelly* kangaroo, still coughing from her dust.

"Come on, *itl*! Let's find the elephants," said *ed*.

Just then, *itl* looked over his shoulder. "Run, *ed*!" he yelled. "A wild animal with long horns is running right for us. We'll be killed!"

ed looked back as he started to run. But when he saw who it was, he laughed and stopped running. "That's *ysabel* (*ee-sa-bel*). She's a yak. She was born in a far-off place called Tibet. She lived high on a mountain where it's snowy all the time. When she was a baby, she was taken to a zoo in Mexico. They gave her a Spanish name—*ysabel*—and taught her to speak Spanish. But with her fur coat, it was too hot for her at that zoo. So they sent her here, to our zoo. She feels better here, but nobody understands her language. So she just stopped talking."

"Maybe we can teach her to talk to us," said *itl*. "She looks like she wants to be friends."

"I'll try," said *ed*.

ed decided to start with the sound of his alphabet name, *ee*. He stood in front of *ysabel* and made a big wide smile. "*ee*," he said.

ysabel stared at *ed*'s face. Then she made a big smile back and said, "*ee*."

"Hooray for you, *ed*!" shouted *itl*. "You did it! You're teaching her to talk again."

"I know," said *ed*. "And when I've taught her to do that, maybe she'll teach me to speak Spanish."

Then *ed* saw *ysabel*'s name on her sign. "Look, *itl*," he said, "*ysabel*'s initial is easy. You just make *uggy*'s letter and give it a curly tail like *jac*'s letter."

Activity

Write the letter *y* in the air, describing each stroke: "Go straight down and around and up again, just like *uggy*'s letter. Then straight down again and curl it at the bottom, like *jac*'s letter." Ask the children to make the sound as they write the letter in the air with you; repeat several times.

Distribute the tear-out section of *my itl book* Activity 22. Demonstrate the steps in drawing *ysabel* on a large sheet of newsprint and have the children complete their drawing.

Draw *ysabel*'s head, body, and feet as shown.

Then add the talking balloon and write *ysabel*'s letter in it as you say the sound.

Tell children to write several more of *ysabel*'s letter below the picture. Then have them color *ysabel*.

Check Point

As children are completing their drawing, ask each child to make *ysabel*'s sound and to write the letter.

Record individual performance on the Progress Checklist.

Extended Activities

1. Distribute *my itl books* and crayons. Have children turn to page 22. Tell children to write *ysabel*'s letter in the talking balloon as they say her sound and then to color *ysabel*.

2. Distribute Activity Sheet 38, crayons, and scissors. Have children color and cut out *ysabel*. Then help them attach the cutout to a folded strip of construction paper or a wooden stick, to make a stick puppet. The puppets may be used to enact the story.

3. Add the new sound and letter to the activities you've already established: Tello game, Look-and-Do strips, feely boxes, magnetic letters, Hop-Spell game.

4. Teach children the hand sign for the letter *y*.

5. Have children form the letter *y* with their body, saying the sound as they make the letter.

6. Choose volunteers to replay the story, either pantomiming it or dramatizing it using their own words.

7. Distribute newsprint, pencils, and crayons. Dictate sentences using the letter *y* in both beginning and ending positions. Emphasize the /ee/ sound.

> is it a *y*ak? *y*es, it is.
> is it a *y*ak? no, it is _____. (Point to a child whose name ends in *y* and dictate the name; help with spelling if necessary.)
> this is *y*umm*y*. It is a _____. (Let children complete the sentence.)

Have children read and illustrate their sentences.

LESSON 53

Objective To make the /y/ sound, as in *my*, and to distinguish it from the /y/ sound in *happy*.

Understandings Children's first independent writings are usually descriptions of personal experiences. They need to be able to discriminate between the frequently used words *me* and *my*. The second sound for the letter *y* and the rule that the letter *y* represents the *i* sound on the end of single-syllable words should be taught before children begin independent writing.

Materials

itl puppet
Character Cards 1, 13, 23
crayons
newsprint—one 12″ x 15″ sheet per child
soft-lead pencils, one per child

Story

Display the character cards as you tell the story.

itl and ysabel

itl and *ed* were still trying to teach *ysabel* yak to talk.

"Let me try now," said *itl*. "Maybe she can learn to make my last name. It's my alphabet name. You say it like this: *ah-ee.*" *itl* stood right in front of *ysabel* and opened his mouth wide, "ahhhhhhhhhh." She opened her mouth and said it too, "ahhhhhhhhhh."

"Good, *ysabel*," said *itl*. "That's the first part. Now we'll do the last part—*ee.* You already know how to say *ee.*"

ysabel opened her mouth big for *ah*. Then she made the smile sound *ee*. She did it again and again: "*ah-ee ah-ee ah-ee.*"

itl said. "You are learning fast, *ysabel*. Now you can make two sounds."

Then *itl* reminded *ed* that they had to find the elephants while it was still daytime. They said good-bye to *ysabel*. *ed* promised to stop by again to teach her a new sound.

Activity

Ask children to make the new sound *ysabel* learned, *ah-ee*, reminding them that it is the same as *itl*'s alphabet name. Then have them make *ysabel*'s first sound, the sound of *ed*'s alphabet name.

Make the following two lists on the board, one for each sound of the letter *y*. Read the lists aloud with the children as you run your finger under each word. Then ask children if they can guess the difference between the lists: one list has

186

long words and one list has short words. Point out that the length of words is sometimes a clue to which sound to use.

y as *ee* (sound in long words)	*y* as *i* (sound in short words)
mommy	my
daddy	sky
funny	dry
happy	by
Jimmy	fry

Give children newsprint and pencils. Dictate sentences that include words in which the letter *y* represents the *i* sound.

this is my _____. (Let children add their own word.)

the sand is dry.

the sun is in the sky.

the man can fry the fish.

Have children illustrate their sentences.

Check Point

Go from child to child to check sentences. Ask children to read their sentences; help them discover and correct any writing errors.

Record individual performance on the Progress Checklist.

Objective To recognize the letter *w*, to say its sound, as in *few*, and to write the letter correctly.

Understandings A vowel is a speech sound produced without occluding, diverting, or obstructing the flow of air from the lungs. In English, the letter *w* is always produced the same way. This letter is simply another way to write the sound already introduced as /oo/ in the octopus stories and the long sound for the letter *u*, as in bl*u*e. The letter *w* clarifies this sound graphically. While no one pronounces *wet* as "wuh-et," some adults incorrectly add an *uh* to this speech sound in isolation. This letter makes only *one* sound (/oo/), regardless of its position in the word (*wow, twin*). Listen carefully and you can hear it on the end of *now* and even *snow*.

Following the Norman conquest of England in the eleventh century, the Norman scribes had particular problems with this sound. The Anglo Saxons used a special character, looking something like a fat *P*, to represent it. They called it *wyn*. The Normans did not want to add another letter to their Latin-based alphabet. They had already adopted the two-vowel system for indicating a long vowel sound. They, therefore, doubled the *u* to indicate its long sound /oo/ in special words. The double *u* was joined to indicate a separation from the adjoining vowels. Thus, middle English *cou* became *cow*.

The Latin *duo* was pronounced by the French as a single vowel (*deux*). The Norman scribes changed *deux* to *tw* for *two*, then added the final *o* to satisfy the established convention that every syllable in English must include an *a, e, i, o,* or *u*.

Forming the letter *w* with four diagonals moving in different directions is too difficult for young children. The rounded *w*—made with two joined *u*'s— is easier and faster. It is also a better foundation for the cursive form and makes more sense to young children (a "double u" should look like a double *u*, not a double *v*).

Materials

itl puppet
Audiocassette, Side 2, "*willy worm*"
Character Cards 1, 13, 24
my itl book Activity 23, one per child
black writing crayons, one per child
crayons
newsprint—one large, easel-sized sheet
black, felt-tipped pen

Story

Display the character cards as you either tell the story or play the recording.

willy worm

itl and *ed* were just leaving *ysabel* yak when they heard someone making loud noises behind them. "WOW! WOWEE! WHOOPEE! WHAMMY!"

"I know who that is," said *itl*. "That's my noisy cousin, *willy* worm. He always makes that *oo* sound when he's excited. But what's he doing here?"

They turned a corner and there they saw a wiggly worm selling tickets for merry-go-round rides.

"Hi, *itl*!" said *willy*. "What are you doing here?"

itl told *willy* about *ed* running away from the zoo and about all their adventures bringing him back.

Then *willy* told *ed* that he had a problem too. One morning when he was very young, he had been caught by an early bird. The bird carried him up in the sky and then accidently dropped him! *willy*'s back had been broken in two places.

itl told *willy* that *ed* had learned how to write most of the letters of the alphabet.

ed looked at *willy*. Then he wrote *willy*'s letter in the dust.

"Hey, that looks just like me!" laughed *willy*. "Wow! Imagine that! An elephant who can write. Wowee!"

Then *ed* and *itl* went on in search of the elephants. But *itl* promised to come back and visit his cousin another day and to buy a ticket for the merry-go-round.

Activity

Ask children to make *willy*'s sound (/oo/). Then write the letter *w* in the air with the children. Repeat several times, saying the sound as you write the letter.

Distribute the tear-out section of *my itl book* Activity 23 and crayons. Demonstrate the steps in drawing *willy* on a sheet of newsprint as children complete their drawing.

Draw *willy*'s letter, head, and body, as shown.

Then add a talking balloon and write *willy*'s letter in it as you say his sound.

Have children write several more of *willy*'s letter below the picture and then color *willy*.

Check Point

As children are completing their drawing, ask each child to say *willy*'s sound and to write the letter.

Record individual performance on the Progress Checklist.

Extended Activities

1. Distribute *my itl books* and crayons. Tell children to turn to page 23. Then tell them to write *willy*'s letter in the talking balloon as they say his sound and then to color *willy*.

2. Distribute Activity Sheet 39, crayons, and scissors. Tell children to color and cut out *willy*. Then help them attach the cutout to a folded strip of construction paper or a wooden stick, to make a stick puppet. The puppets may be used to enact the story.

3. Add the sound and letter *w* to the activities you've already established: Tello game, Look-and-Do strips, boxes of objects, feely boxes, magnetic letters, Hop-Spell game.

4. Teach children the hand sign for the letter *w*.

5. Choose volunteers to replay the story, either pantomiming it or dramatizing it using their own words.

6. Give children newsprint, pencils, and crayons. Dictate words with the letter *w* in the beginning, middle, and ending positions (*wow, now, wet, wig, win, wind, twin*). Have children repeat the words, write them, and then illustrate them.

LESSON 55

Objective To recognize the letter *v*, to say its sound, as in *have*, and to write the letter correctly.

Understandings This letter is the twin sound to *f*. It is produced the same way, except the larynx is activated. Children who speak Spanish at home may need some help because the Spanish /b/ and /v/ are so similar. Try to teach them to "pop" the /b/ but let the /v/ slide out. Otherwise they will be confused by dictation games. For example, these children may write *ban* instead of *van*.

The first stroke of this letter, the diagonal downward and toward the right side, is the last of the letter strokes to develop. The second slide, up toward the right and away from the body, is easy to make; it is found in toddler's earliest scribbles. Because of its simplicity, children tend to make the second diagonal rapidly and bend it into a curve. Children may need to be told that the wings of the vulture are straight. It is standing, not flying.

Materials

 itl puppet
 Audiocassette, Side 2, "*victor vulture*"
 Character Cards 1, 13, 25
 my itl book Activity 24, one per child
 black writing crayons, one per child
 crayons
 newsprint—one large, easel-sized sheet
 black, felt-tipped pen

Story

Display the character cards as you either tell the story or play the recording.

victor vulture

itl and *ed* left *willy* worm at the merry-go-round. *ed* was getting more and more excited about getting home. "The elephant house is way over there," he said. "First we go by the bird cages."

"Look at that enormous bird in there," said *itl*. "He looks scary."

"Oh, that's *victor* vulture," said *ed*. "He does look scary, but he can't even bite. His top beak doesn't fit on his bottom beak. That's why he makes that noise: v-v-v-v-v. The zoo keeper takes him to the zoo dentist. The dentist is fixing his bite so he can chew better."

itl felt sorry for the big bird who couldn't eat much with his beak the way it was. So *itl* gave the bird his recipe for violet-velvet vanilla cream custard—a food that's delicious, and easy to chew.

While *victor* memorized the recipe so that he could tell the zoo keeper about it, *ed* looked at the name on *victor*'s cage. He found it easy to make *victor*'s letter: a down slide, followed by an up slide. At first he made it too fast, so it looked like *victor* was flying. But with just a little care and practice, *ed* could write it perfectly.

Then *ed* and *itl* started off again, with *victor* still muttering, "Violet-velvet vanilla cream custard! v-v-v-v-v!"

Activity

Ask children to make *victor*'s sound. Show them how to put their top teeth on their bottom lip (like *victor*'s beak) and make his noise. Ask them if they can feel why *victor* couldn't bite with his teeth in this position.

Write *victor*'s letter in the air, describing the strokes. Then ask children to write his letter in the air with you; remind them that the up slide is straight. Repeat several times, saying the sound as you make the letter.

Distribute the tear-out section of *my itl book* Activity 24 and black crayons. Demonstrate the steps in drawing *victor* on a large sheet of newsprint as children complete their drawing.

Draw *victor*'s letter, body, head, wings, and feet as shown.

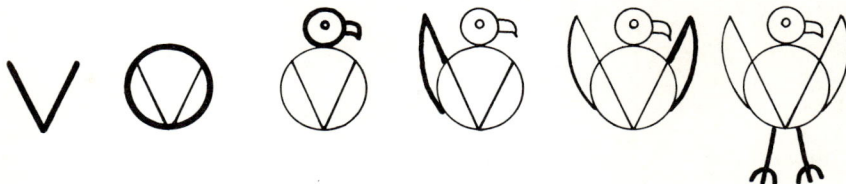

Then add a talking balloon and write the letter in the balloon as you say the sound.

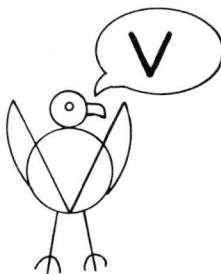

Tell children to write several of *victor*'s letter below the picture and then to color *victor*.

Check Point

As children are completing their drawing, ask each child to make the sound and to write the letter.

Record individual performance on the Progress Checklist.

Extended Activities

1. Distribute *my itl books* and crayons. Have children turn to page 24. Tell them to write *victor*'s letter in the talking balloon and to say his sound and then to color *victor*.

2. Distribute Activity Sheet 40, crayons, and scissors. Have children color and cut out *victor*. Then help them attach the cutout to a strip of folded construction paper or a wooden stick, to make a stick puppet. The puppets may be used to enact the story.

3. Add the /v/ sound and letter to the activities you've already established: Tello game, Look-and-Do strips, feely boxes, magnetic letters, Hop-Spell game.

4. Teach the hand sign for the letter *v*.

5. Have children make the letter *v* with their body, saying the sound as they make the letter.

6. Choose volunteers to play *itl*, *ed*, and *victor*. Have them replay the story as you retell it, or dramatize it using their own words.

7. Give children newsprint and pencils. Dictate words with the new sound; for example: *van, vest*. Explain Spelling Rule 8: English words never end in the letter *v*. Demonstrate by writing these words on the board: *give, have, live, dive, cave*. (See *Writing Is Child's Play*, Appendix B.)

8. Send home Parent Letter 12.

LESSON 56

Objective To recognize the letter x, to say its sound, as in *six*, and to write the letter correctly.

Understandings This letter, like v, begins with the diagonal downward and toward the right. Because the second stroke is easier to make, young children tend to reverse the order of the strokes. This is not a serious error because the letter is not distorted. Also, this letter is so rare in English that a distorted x will not make one's handwriting illegible. The difficulty for some children is aiming for the middle of the first diagonal. Putting a dot on the line will help some children in their aim. Very uncoordinated children tend to avoid the diagonal (turning x into a vertical-horizontal cross t). Writing x's in the squares on graph paper, where the diagonals can be written from corner to corner will help these children. The letter x is used to represent three speech sounds in English (/ks/ as in *box*, /gs/ as in *exam*, and /z/ as in *xylophone*). The first sound is by far the most common. Beginners don't need to learn the other two. The x appears most often as an ending sound in primary reading and writing tasks.

Materials

> *itl* puppet
> Audiocassette, Side 2, "*max the kissing bug*"
> Character Cards 1, 13, 26
> *my itl book* Activity 25, one per child
> black writing crayons, one per child
> crayons
> newsprint—one large, easel-sized sheet
> black, felt-tipped pen

Story

Display the character cards as you tell the story or play the recording.

max the kissing bug

ed and *itl* left the bird cages and were almost to the little train.

"Let's take a train ride," said *itl*. "I'm tired from all this walking."

"No," said *ed*. "I want to get to the elephant house."

All of a sudden they heard a noise like this: "*ks-ks-ks.*"

itl looked up. "What's making that noise? Yipes! He's coming right at me! I hope he doesn't sting!"

A bug landed right on *itl*'s head, saying: "*ks-ks-ks.*"

"Oh, no, he doesn't sting," said *ed*. "He kisses. That's *max*, the kissing bug. He likes to kiss everybody. He says *kiss, kiss, kiss* so fast it sounds like *ks-ks-ks.*"

After *max* had kissed *itl* a few times, he flew over to a fence and folded his wings so that *itl* and *ed* could see the design on his back.

"That's interesting," said *itl*. "The mark on his back is the letter for his sound: *ks-ks-ks.*"

"Is it really?" *ed* asked. "Why, I can make that!" And he wrote the letter in the dust. Then he noticed something. "Look over there, *itl*. That sign on top of the post by the train tracks has *max*'s letter on it."

"That's right," said *itl*. "His letter also stands for *railroad crossing.*" Then he smiled. "And it stands for a kiss when you write it at the end of a letter."

With that, they waved good-bye to *max* and he blew them kisses: "*ks-ks-ks.*"

Activity

Ask children to make *max*'s kissing sound. Then write the letter in the air, asking children to do it with you. Say the sound as you write the letter.

Distribute the tear-out section of *my itl book* Activity 25 and black crayons. Demonstrate the steps in drawing *max* on a large sheet of newsprint as the children complete their drawing.

Draw *max*'s letter, body, face, and wings as shown.

Then add a talking balloon and write the letter in the balloon as you say the sound.

Tell children to write several more of *max*'s letter below the picture and then to color *max*.

Check Point

As children are completing their drawing, ask each child to make the sound and to write the letter.

Record individual performance on the Progress Checklist.

Extended Activities

1. Distribute *my itl books* and crayons. Have children turn to page 25. Tell them to write *max*'s letter in the talking balloon and to say his sound. Then have them color *max*.

2. Distribute Activity Sheet 41, crayons, and scissors. Tell children to color and cut out *max*. Then help them attach the cutout to a folded strip of construction paper or to a wooden stick, to make a stick puppet. The puppets may be used to enact the story.

3. Add the /x/ sound and letter to the activities you've already established: Tello game, Look-and-Do strips, box of objects, feely box, magnetic letters, Hop-Spell game.

4. Teach children the hand sign for the letter x.

5. Have children form the letter x with their body, saying the sound as they make the letter.

6. Choose volunteers to play *itl, ed,* and *max* and replay the story as you retell it or dramatize it using their own words.

7. Give children newsprint and pencils. Dictate sentences with the letter x in them. Remind children to use the new letter, not *c* or *k,* in these sentences.
Have children repeat each sentence and then write it.

> the fox is in the box.
> the six is next to the seven.
> the man can fix it.
> *max* is at the exit.

Have children illustrate their sentences. While they are drawing, help them read the sentences.

8. Give children paper and pencils. Dictate a short letter to a special person. Show children how to put x's on the bottom to represent kisses.

9. Discuss the meaning of the x on the signs at railroad crossings.

10. Discuss the meaning of the x as a marking on worksheets or answer forms. Make up a simple worksheet to show children how to mark a correct answer with an x. For example:

> a bird can fly   yes   ☐
>   no   ☐
> a pup is a cat   yes   ☐
>   no   ☐

Objective To recognize the letter *z*, to say its sound, and to write the letter correctly.

Understandings This sound has already been introduced with the letter *s*. The letter *s* represents the sound for /z/ in written English forty times more often than the letter *z* (Dewey 1970). The letter *s* is used for this sound usually on the end or in the middle of words (i*s*, sci*s*sors). The letter *z* usually represents this sound in the beginning of words (*z*oo).

This is the only letter of the alphabet that begins with a "resting" line. Associating it with the number 7, which has already been taught, will help prevent reversal.

Materials

itl puppet

Audiocassette, Side 2, "*zippy zebra*"

Character Cards 1, 13, 27

my itl book Activity 26, one per child

black writing crayons, one per child

crayons

newsprint—one 12″ x 15″ sheet per child; one large, easel-sized sheet

black, felt-tipped pen

Story

Display the character cards as you either tell the story or play the recording.

zippy zebra

Just before they came to the elephant house, *ed* and *itl* walked past the zebras.

"Look at them," said *ed*. "There are seven of them in this zoo."

"You're right," said *itl*. This one near the fence seems to be sleeping standing up."

"That's *zippy*," said *ed*. "See his stripes? He looks like he has zippers all over. That's why we call him *zippy*. Listen to him snore."

zippy was making noises like this: "z-z-z-z-z-z-z-z-z-z-z-z-z-z-z-z-z-z."

"Look, *itl*," he said. "*zippy*'s letter starts just like a seven. And there are seven zebras. If I remember that, it will help me remember how to write *zippy*'s letter." *ed* made a 7 in the dust and then added a line at the bottom. "See?" he said.

itl said, "You're so clever, *ed*. And now I'll tell you something. You know how to make every letter that I know about. You know enough to write every word in the world if you listen to the word and think about the sounds."

"Wow!" said *ed*. "Every word in the world!"

Then *ed* remembered how much he wanted to show the elephants what he had learned. So *ed* and *itl* moved on toward the elephant house—quietly, so they wouldn't disturb *zippy*, who was still sleeping: "z-z-z-z."

Activity

Write the letter in the air. Then ask the children to write the letter in the air with you, saying the sound as they make the letter; repeat several times.

Distribute the tear-out section of *my itl book* Activity 26 and black crayons. Demonstrate the steps in drawing *zippy* on a large sheet of newsprint as children complete their drawing.

Draw *zippy*'s letter and body as shown.

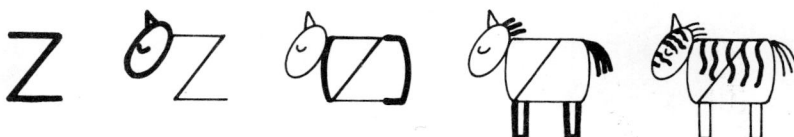

Then add a talking balloon and write the letter in the balloon as you say the sound.

Then tell children to write several more of *zippy*'s letter below the picture.

When children have completed the drawing, give each child a sheet of newsprint and a pencil. Tell children that when we hear this sound on the end of words we usually use *sissy*'s letter. When we hear it in the beginning of words, we usually use *zippy*'s letter.

Dictate sentences that have the sound in the two positions; have children repeat each sentence and then write it. Remind children to think: "Where is the /z/?"

*z*ap, bang, pow, it *is* a _____. (Encourage children to finish the sentences.)
*z*ip, *z*ip, it i*s* a fast _____.
i*s* it hi*s*? yes
zzzzzzzzzzzzz it i*s z*ippy.

Tell children to read the sentences to themselves and then to illustrate them.

Check Point

While children are completing their drawings, go from child to child and ask each one to make the sound and to write the letter.

Record individual performance on the Progress Checklist.

Extended Activities

1. Distribute *my itl books* and crayons. Have children turn to page 26. Tell them to write *zippy*'s letter in the talking balloon and to say his sound and then to color *zippy*.

2. Distribute Activity Sheet 42, crayons, and scissors. Tell children to color and cut out *zippy*. Then help them attach the cutout to a folded strip of construction paper or to a wooden stick, to make a stick puppet. The puppets may be used to enact the story.

3. Add the /z/ sound and letter to activities you've already established: Tello game, Look-and-Do strips, feely boxes, magnetic letters, Hop-Spell game.

4. Teach the hand sign for the letter *z*.

5. Have children form the letter *z* with their body, saying the sound as they make the letter.

6. Choose volunteers to play *itl*, *ed*, and *zippy*. Have them replay the story as you retell it, or dramatize it using their own words.

UNIT 8
ALPHABET ORDER AND CAPITAL LETTERS

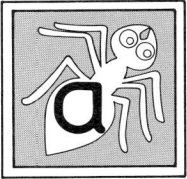

lphabet order and capital letters are the focus of the final unit of the *itl Early Writing Program*. At this point, children know how to write all twenty-six lowercase letters, and how to record all of the sounds used in everyday speech.

LESSON 58

Objective To write the alphabet in order.

Understandings By this time, children who have been taught with the *itl Early Writing Program* should be writing well enough independently that alphabet letter names won't confuse them.

Materials

itl puppet

Activity Sheet 43, one copy per child

Audiocassette, Side 2, *"ed and the alphabet"*

Character Card 28

pencils

Story

Display Character Card 28 as you either tell the story or play the recording.

ed and the alphabet

"See, *itl*," said *ed*. "There's the sign that says 'elephants.' It starts just like my name, *ed*."

They opened the gate and went inside.

"I can hardly wait," said *itl*, "till you show these elephants how smart you are!"

Three of the elephants were showing off for visitors, playing "Follow-the-Leader." The elephant in front looked up.

"Hey, look, fellows," he called. "*ed*'s home."

"Wait till he shows you the trick he learned," said *itl*.

One of the elephants stood on his back feet. "What kind of a trick did you learn, *ed*? You'd only trip if you tried this one. And who is that funny-looking character with you?"

itl spoke up. "I'm *itl*. I found *ed* when he was lost. He has learned to write all the alphabet letters. Show them, *ed*!"

ed picked up a little stick in his trunk. Then he found a smooth place in the dust in the elephant pen. He wrote all the letters, starting with *anny*'s letter and ending with *zippy*'s.

The other elephants were amazed.

"Show us how to do it too," said the elephant who was standing on his back feet.

"It takes a long time to learn how to write all the letters," said *ed*. "But you can do it if you just learn them one at a time like I did."

itl looked at the elephants. "It's easy to learn the alphabet song. I'll show you how to sing it right now. It goes like this: (Have *itl* ask the children to help him sing.)

a b c d e f g
h i j k l m n o p
q r s t u v
w x y z."

Activity

Say the alphabet in order with the children. Then ask individual children or small groups of children to say it. If you discover a number of children who need help naming letters, teach the letters in groups according to their name sounds.

Those that rhyme with *e*—*c, d, g, p, t, v, z, b*
Those that rhyme with *a*—*jay, kay*
Those that begin with *ed*'s beginning sound—*ef, el, em, en, es, ex*
Those in the farm song—*a, e, i, o, u*
The tricky ones—*h, q, r, w, y*

Give children Activity Sheet 43 and pencils for writing the entire alphabet in correct sequence, without letters to copy.

If writing twenty-six letters from memory is too much for some children, take it in groups, like the alphabet song:

a b c d e f g
h i j k l m n o p
q r s t u v
w x y z

Remind children to sing as they write so they are constantly proofreading. Have children write their names on their paper.

Check Point

Review the completed activity sheets. Record individual performance on the Progress Checklist.

Objective To recognize, use, and write capital letters correctly.

Understandings The capital letters are introduced in groups, according to writing difficulty. They should be introduced one group at a time, in separate sessions.

> Capitals that are exactly the same as their lowercase counterparts: C O S U V X Z
>
> Capitals that are made with only vertical and horizontal lines and are oriented toward the right: E F H I L T
>
> Capitals oriented toward the left: G J Q
>
> Capitals that begin with a stick and add a right curve: B D P R
>
> Capitals that consist of diagonal strokes: A K M N W Y

Materials

> *itl* puppet
> Activity Sheets 44-69, one copy of each per child
> Character Cards 1 and 13
> crayons
> newsprint—one 12″ x 15″ sheet per child; large, easel-sized sheets
> black, felt-tipped pen
> soft-lead pencils

Story

Display the character cards as you tell the story.

itl and ed say good-bye

itl said good-bye to *ed.* It was time for him to go home. *ed* gave *itl* a big hug with his trunk.

"Now that I can write letters," he said, "the elephants don't laugh at me anymore. Thank you, *itl,* for showing me how to write."

On his way out of the zoo, *itl* saw a gift shop. He said to himself, "Maybe they have some souvenirs I can take home to my friends." He looked at the T-shirts, the stuffed animals, and the postcards.

Then, he found something just right. He found some balloons. Each one had a capital letter on it. He decided it was time for the animals to learn to write their names starting with a capital letter. So he bought twenty-six balloons; one for himself, and one for each of his friends.

He made up a rhyme for each one so he wouldn't forget any of them.

Before leaving the zoo, *itl* gave *ed, ysabel, victor, kelly, max, zippy,* and *willy* their balloons. Then he tied the other balloons around his middle to take home. Whoops! The balloons took him away up in the sky! "This beats walking," he called. "I'll be home in a hurry. Good-bye everybody!"

Activity

Distribute pencils and the activity sheets for one group of letters at a time, as follows:

> Activity Sheets 44-50 for letters C O S U V X Z
> Activity Sheets 51-56 for letters E F H I L T
> Activity Sheets 57-59 for letters G J Q
> Activity Sheets 60-63 for letters B D P R
> Activity Sheets 64-69 for letters A K M N W Y

For each letter, read the rhyme to the children and then read it again together. On newsprint, show children how to make the letter stroke by stroke. Then tell children to make the letters on each page, following the arrows. Children may color the characters on each page. Save the sheets until all twenty-six letters are completed. Help children put the sheets in alphabetic order to make a take-home alphabet book.

Check Point

Give children newsprint and pencils. Dictate the sounds and ask children to write the capital letter for each sound.

Record individual performance on the Progress Checklist.

Extended Activities

1. For each group of letters: Discuss the use of capital letters at the beginning of sentences, beginning of names, and in titles. Show children how to write the names of children in the group beginning with the particular capitals being taught.

Give children newsprint and pencils. Dictate phrases or sentences that show the use of capitals. For example:

> Can *uggy* quack?
> The Three Little Pigs
> The End

2. Send home Parent Letter 13.

Follow-Up Activities

For regular practice of skills taught in the *itl Early Writing Program*, have children begin journal writing. Each day, ask children to draw a picture of a personal experience and then to write about it. For example, "I had an apple for lunch," or "I like to wear my red dress." Encourage children to use invented spelling for words they are not sure how to spell. Tell children to use their ears to help them write. Gradually add simple spelling rules and the "outlaw words" that must be memorized. (See "Spelling" and "Original Composition" in *Writing Is Child's Play.*)

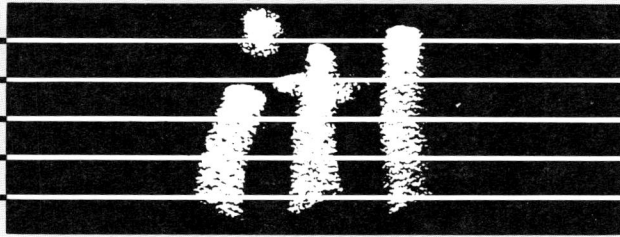

APPENDIXES

Appendix A   Signing Alphabet*

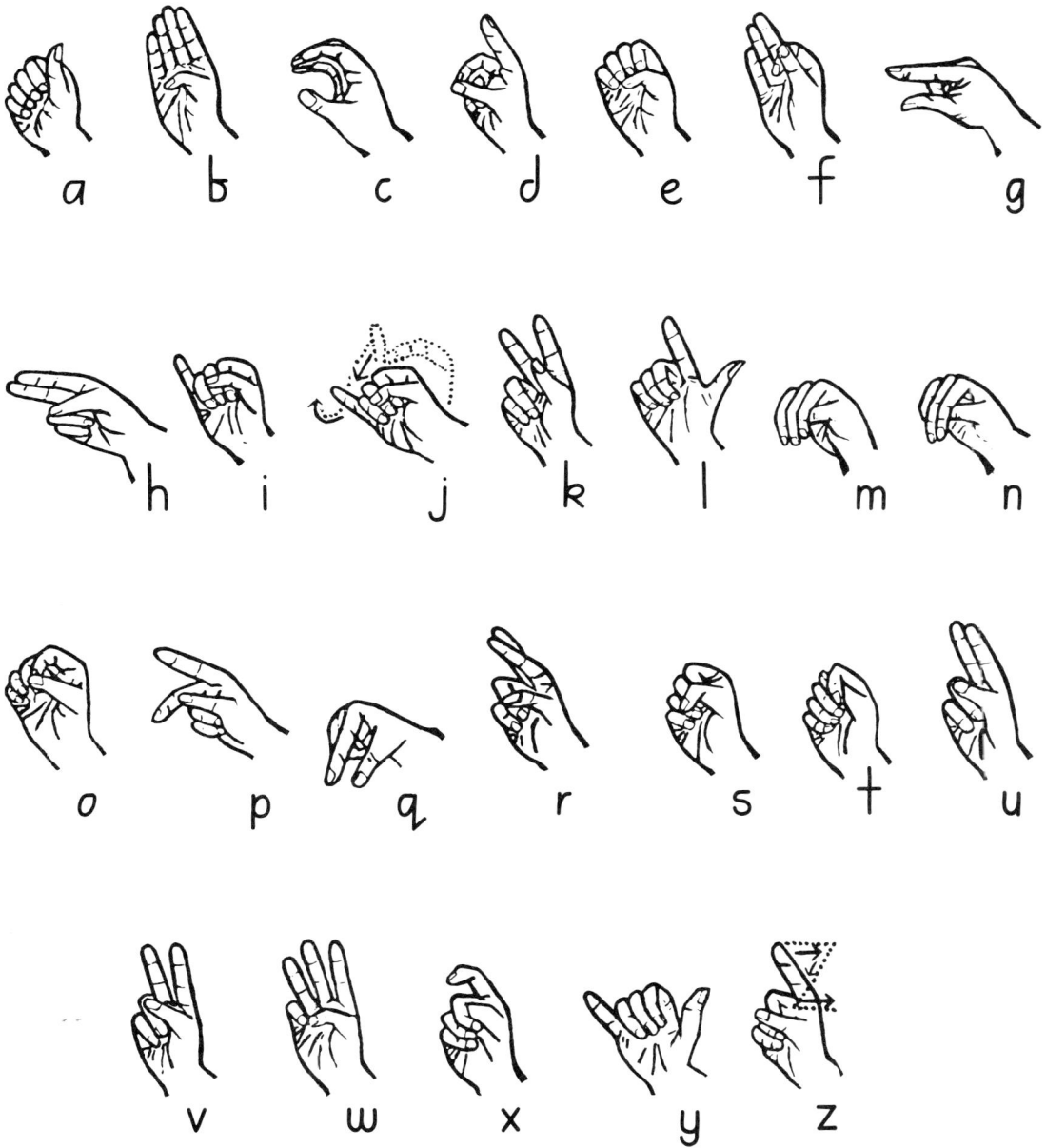

a   b   c   d   e   f   g

h   i   j   k   l   m   n

o   p   q   r   s   t   u

v   w   x   y   z

*American Manual Alphabet, courtesy of D.E.A.F., Inc.

Appendix B   Materials

1 *Writing Is Child's Play*

1 Lesson Guide

1 *itl* **Puppet**

28 Character Cards

1 *itl inchworm*	15 *rusty rooster*
2 *til turtle*	16 *nosey nag*
3 *lit ladybug*	17 *hamilton hound*
4 *jac jack rabbit*	18 *molly mosquito*
5 *cat caterpillar*	19 *piggy*
6 *anny ant*	20 *bud bird*
7 *dotty dalmatian*	21 *coo-coo quail*
8 *gus grasshopper*	22 *kelly kangaroo*
9 *the talent contest*	23 *ysabel yak*
10 *fred frog*	24 *willy worm*
11 *sissy snake*	25 *victor vulture*
12 *olly octopus*	26 *max the kissing bug*
13 *ed elephant*	27 *zippy zebra*
14 *uggy duck*	28 *ed and the alphabet*

1 *my itl book*

1 Audiocassette

Side A

itl inchworm	*gus grasshopper*
til turtle	*the talent contest*
lit ladybug	*fred frog*
jac jack rabbit	*sissy snake*
cat caterpillar	*olly octopus*
anny ant	*ed elephant*
dotty dalmatian	*uggy duck*

Side B

rusty rooster	*kelly kangaroo*
nosey nag	*ysabel yak*
hamilton hound	*willy worm*
molly mosquito	*victor vulture*
piggy	*max the kissing bug*
bud bird	*zippy zebra*
coo-coo quail	*ed and the alphabet*

84 Blackline Masters

Progress Checklist
Lesson Planning and Evaluation Form
69 Activity Sheets
13 Parent Letters

1 *itl* **Poster**

54 Tello Cards

Sample Writing Materials

1 black writing crayon	1 triangular plastic gripper
1 pencil	1 writing slate

Appendix C   Letter and Sound Chart

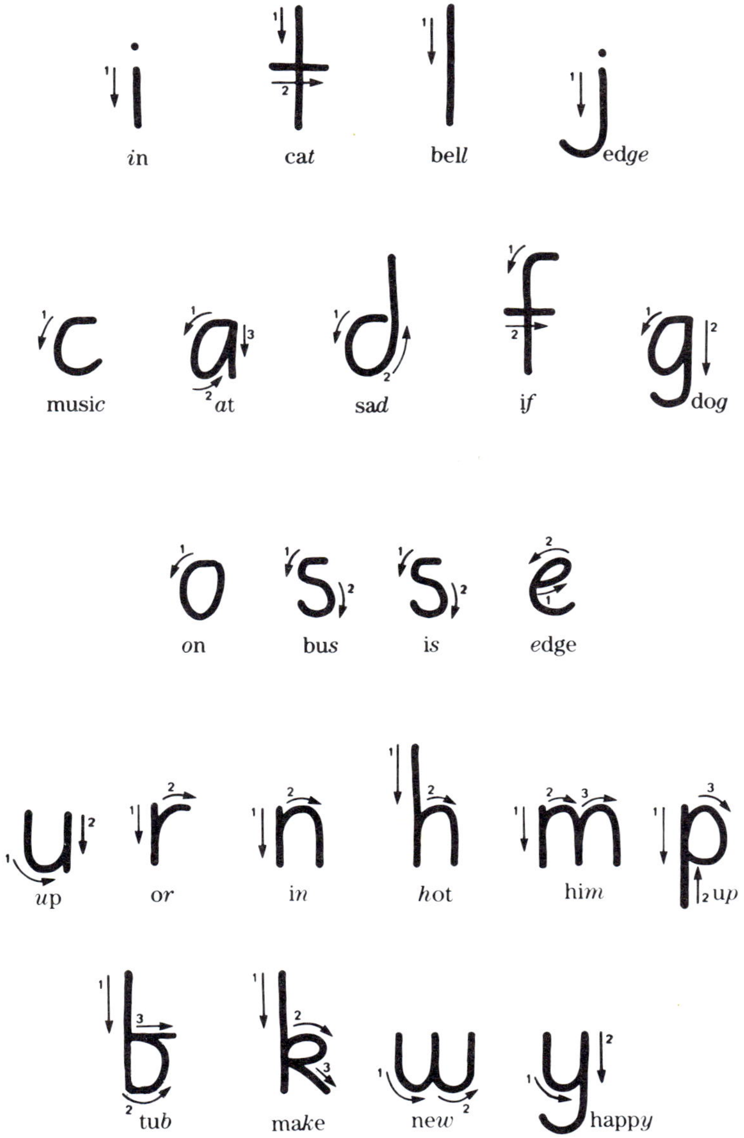

i
in

t
cat

l
be*ll*

j
e*dge*

c
musi*c*

a
at

d
sa*d*

f
if

g
do*g*

o
on

s
bu*s*

s
is

e
edge

u
up

r
or

n
in

h
hot

m
hi*m*

p
up

b
tu*b*

k
ma*k*e

w
ne*w*

y
happ*y*

qu _quick_   ng _bang_   th _this_   ch _itch_

sh _wish_   th _thin_

v _have_   x _box_   z _buzz_